A NEW WAY

A NEW WAY

EMBRACING THE PARADOX
AS WE LEAD AND SERVE

MATTHEW DOWD

ANAM CARA

COPYRIGHT © 2017 MATTHEW DOWD
All rights reserved.

A NEW WAY
Embracing the Paradox as We Lead and Serve

ISBN   978-1-5445-0032-4   *Paperback*
       978-1-5445-0033-1   *Ebook*

CONTENTS

PILGRIMAGE
FROM A DREAM

The poet Sandburg wrote, "Nothing happens unless first a dream."

Martin Luther King Jr. had a dream. He gave a pointed and memorable speech on that dream, and ultimately, his dream of civil rights for African Americans became a reality. It took a vision, relentless hard work, courage, focus, stumbles and falls, and a community of people to make it happen through many avenues in politics, business, and faith.

Not all dreams are the same, but they all are trying to convey some message or truth. Sometimes we awaken from dreams, wipe our eyes, put our feet on the floor, and just move onto what we had already planned for that day. We forget that we even had a dream and can't recall a single detail.

Then there are times we retain the dream, and it might even echo within us for the rest of that day or the days to come, gently speaking to us or just passing through us as a fantasy experience—sometimes good, sometimes bad. Even with those dreams, though, often we just keep walking through the day.

But then there are those dreams that we awake from and we know clearly that we must take what they say and act on it. I woke from one of those dreams a few years ago, and a couple of months later, I stepped off a plane in India by myself with just a backpack. I think it is the time the dream hits us and where we are in our lives that determines what we are supposed to do with that dream. Or maybe we just take a chance that the dream is God or the universe speaking to us, and we can't ignore it.

In 2007, after helping George W. Bush get elected and then reelected president of the United States, I became convinced, even though I believe him to be a good man and I respect him, that the promise of his presidency of bridging the divides in America and getting past the dysfunction of bitter partisanship had become less probable. I decided I must speak out and say that I had become disillusioned and disheartened. I felt I needed to do it publicly, because I had been a public advocate for him for five years. This was a difficult decision. Doing so, I lost friends I'd thought I could count on and business clients who now no longer wanted to be associated with me. I also felt that

I was jettisoning a dream of rising in politics that I'd had since I first got hooked as a twelve-year-old in Michigan on summer vacation watching the Watergate hearings.

Not long after this public break with President Bush, and being only a few years from my second divorce and the loss of a daughter and a son, I began to feel that I needed to take a trip alone—completely solo. I was also reading a lot on different religions and faiths, comparing and contrasting them, and I was trying to understand or interpret all of that in my life. I guess it was part of the journey I had been on for the past few years. I felt I should go somewhere and just be. It was in that context that I had a dream of walking in the path of the five major spiritual faiths (Judaism, Buddhism, Hinduism, Islam, and Christianity).

The dream wasn't overly specific. Just a notion to go on a pilgrimage by myself to the holy places of these faiths, to see what I might see or learn what I might learn. I decided to start where Hinduism had begun in India and to finish in Assisi, where my personal hero Saint Francis had lived and changed the world. Where I would go in between was a mystery to me when I awoke.

So I did what any person in the twenty-first century would do: I got on the web and began to search. I learned quickly that I would not be going to Mecca or Medina (two of the major holy spots of Islam), since you have to be a Muslim to enter those places. I could go see ancient mosques in India, however, and I would go to Jerusalem (another holy spot for Islam as well as for Christianity and Judaism). Also, I knew that a key place in the world of Islam was Turkey, so I added that to my list.

I figured out that Nepal was the birthplace of Buddha (in Lumbini), and, as the story goes, he attained enlightenment in a small town in rural India. I needed to go to Varanasi, on the Ganges River—a very special place for Hinduism. Other key places for Buddhism and Hinduism would be spread throughout various locales in India that I knew I would need (that is a broad use of that term, since "need" is a stretch on a trip like this) to visit.

I would also go to the Sea of Galilee and the place where Jesus delivered his Sermon on the Mount, which had given the world the Beatitudes, a new way to live. And I would fly to Rome, stop by the Vatican, and tour various key places there. Finally, I would take a short train or bus to Assisi.

This was my rough plan based on a dream and a little bit of research on the net. I called the mom of my daughter Josephine (the identical twin sister of the daughter we'd lost) to see, for the six weeks or so that I would be gone, if she could keep Josephine on the weekends that I normally would have had her. She could, though I didn't tell her exactly what I was doing, because at that point my confidence in my plan wasn't solid enough to stand up against being told I was crazy.

My next stop was a call to a travel agent who specializes in this type of international travel. I explained my rough plan to her and wanted to know if it was possible to accomplish my itinerary in less than six weeks—about forty days. Forty days has significance in a number of faiths as a time of preparation for change and reformation. The travel agent said she would check and get back to me, adding that this was the first time anyone had ever asked this. Hmm, part of me thought that was odd, but another part of me thought, "Awesome! Who wants to do normal?"

The travel agent called back a couple of hours later and said that yes, it was possible, but it would be a "total planes, trains, and automobiles" kind of trip. She also said I would need to be ready along the way to call audibles (that's a football term, where you throw out the play at the line of scrimmage and just start over) and that hitchhiking wouldn't be out of the question to get to some spots. I listened to her intently and said, "Book a nonrefundable ticket to New Delhi" on the date I would leave. She did, and I was pretty much locked in.

I knew myself well enough that if I didn't lock myself in as best I could, then things would come up in life that would cause me to cancel or postpone the trip. I would come up with reasons why I shouldn't go or why this trip was crazy. Sometimes you just have to "throw your hat over the fence," as they say, to commit yourself to climbing over to a new spot. This observation was actually the first of many things I learned about life through this trip.

So often if we think too much about all the logistics,

then we don't ever make the leap to do what the voices inside us are telling us to do. Our own cautious, overly logical voice tells us we should be doing something else or that this is a bad idea. I knew that I had to leap—and then the logistics would take care of themselves, or I would figure it out along the way.

I think many of us feel there is something we must do in life, that voices inside us are calling us to live a certain way. But then other people—or we ourselves—stop us from carrying out our calling because of the details. Those callings can include a trip overseas, a decision postponed on a divorce or on asking someone to get married, changing jobs, or even giving someone a dollar on the street corner.

I am not saying in every instance we should just jump at the pulls of our hearts, but I think most of us need to let the heart lead and the head follow. I understand this isn't easy. I say often, as others do, that we should "follow our hearts," but many times we feel our hearts pulling us in two different directions. It is also difficult to determine which one is the heart and which is the head. Or perhaps I care about both these options a lot, and now I feel conflicted and can't choose.

My own advice from trial and error is, in these moments, to sit quietly alone. Stop asking others for advice, and go to your own self for counsel. Play out the decision you have to make, and see what each option feels like. My bet is that one option will give you a sense of relief. You will feel your body relax. The other option will keep you spinning, and your body will tighten. Your physical body will give you a big clue about which way your heart is really pulling you and what is most authentic to you.

But it is key that you do this in quiet and solitude. The answer will come. Maybe not on your timetable, but it will come. Pay attention to what pops up in your path during this decision time. What you see, a book or television show you notice, what some stranger might say to you out of the blue. Try to be open to signals you were not aware of previously.

We will each make mistakes along the way, but at least our lives will be ours. And we can make a different decision later on if we feel that is needed. If we are thoughtful and heartfelt and intentional as we move forward, then clarity will come. But the important thing is to start listening to the voices within us, our dreams, and how those dreams physically affect us. These are the most important voices we will ever hear.

When I got off the plane at the New Delhi airport and walked outside with just a backpack and some thoughts on the pilgrimage ahead, I wasn't prepared for the assault on my senses. I was overwhelmed by the combination of the sight of so many people scurrying about, the noise of the crowd and the traffic, and the smells of the city. It was as if a truck had hit me and I had to recover my footing. I actually set my backpack down to regain my balance and try to adjust. All my senses were completely overwhelmed.

Throughout the trip, I was constantly in a traffic jam or in a sea of people moving about in what seemed like a total haphazard way. Horns were honking, people were pushing, animals were running about, folks on bicycles were fighting for each bit forward, competing with cars, motorcycles, and pedestrians. I had always been in a hurry in my life, trying to get to where I was going as quickly and efficiently as possible, and here in India I realized that if I kept that up, I would either lose my mind or abandon this trip.

I had always been good at pointing out where there was some sort of disorganization and how it could be fixed. No matter if I was in an airport, a grocery line, or a parking lot, or if I was waiting for a table in a restaurant, I couldn't turn this trait off. My patience was thin for what I perceived as disorganization, and unknowingly, I carried my impatience with me when I landed in New Delhi.

I didn't realize that the slow pace and what seemed like a complete lack of organization were a gift until much later on. I didn't want to get an ulcer, and I also was not going to give up, so I began to let go of my own pace and settle into the pace of the present place. To allow where I was and what I was doing to define my speed and destination. When I returned to Austin weeks later, I realized how ridiculous I had been in my ways before. At times, I still try to manage things and speed things up, but this experience from India would root me in a new way.

All that assault on my senses was the real start of this trip, the completion of which would turn out to be one of the most physically and emotionally difficult things I had ever done. I didn't realize I would sleep so little, struggle to find food at times, and search for clean places to use a restroom (which often was just a hole in the open ground). Even finding toilet paper became a big part of my day. By the end of this trip, I had lost fifteen pounds. I was exhausted and emotionally wrenched.

Like many pilgrims from previous centuries who set out on their travels to see sacred sites, I had many thoughts about what I might learn and experience. I expected to be touched by the sacred places and awakened by the amazing structures and monuments along the way. But the most important lesson I took from my trip was unexpected.

In order to get to all these sacred places—key Hindu sites in rural India; such Buddhist historical places as Buddha's birthplace in Lumbini, Nepal, or where he got enlightenment in Bodh Gayh, India; mosques throughout Turkey and India; or the Jewish and Christian holy places in and around Jerusalem—you have to walk a path through people.

You can't experience these sacred places without walking through the most heart-wrenching sea of humanity each step of the way. I walked by and touched children no more than three years old, standing alone begging for money. I saw six-month-old babies lying in the dirt on the outskirts of these sites, crying for food. I witnessed old people who were blind and bent way over trying to get relief by leaning against trees.

I saw people without feet begging with their hands, and I saw people without hands begging with their feet. I saw six-year-olds pushing away four-year-olds so they could get the few coins of charity, because they hadn't had a meal in days. I saw and was touched by every aspect of humanity.

Often we avert our eyes to the beggars in our own streets and make our way to our cool offices and nice lunches. We have been trained to look away from or not look directly at someone asking for something, because it's supposedly the best way to not get accosted or to make our way quickly to where we want to go. But the greatest gift we can give a beggar or a homeless person is that they are seen by someone, that they are recognized as a fellow human.

It is not just beggars whom we don't see or look away from. It is also people in our own lives. Our spouse, our children, our other family members, our friends—we often-times don't see or notice them. Think about the difference in how you feel if you walk into a room and someone's eyes notice you and light up because you are there, as opposed to how you feel if you receive either no look or a glazed-over one as if you didn't exist.

Well, on that trip of mine to sacred sites, there was no possible way I could avert my eyes or avoid the humanity in my path. It took me five or six days before I finally let go of the anxiety and tension in me as I walked through all these people whom Jesus often called our brothers and sisters and just let myself be in the midst of them.

I had to encounter my own internal judgments about all this. I had to examine my own prejudices as I approached people or avoided people. I had to look at myself a number of times in the mirror and shake hands with my own demons. I had to stop moving so fast. I had to stop rushing past people. I had to slow down and try to take it all in.

I began trying to talk to folks. I tried smiling when it seemed right. I began pausing in the midst of these people who were trying to survive just that day. I realized just in the act of seeking out all these religions that this was a big lesson about what truly was holy. You can't get to hardly any of these sacred places without walking through the sadness and tragedy of life. You can't find the beauty of a great cathedral without stepping through lost and starving children.

We each feel there is some holy place on earth we want to visit and see. We realize that in order to experience this holy place, we will need to wade into the midst of men, women, and children who suffer. I couldn't touch the holy waters of the sacred Ganges River without being touched by an old woman scarred by life. Or as I took a wooden boat out on the Ganges, I smelled the primitive fires of folks burning their deceased loved ones on the shore. In the boat not far from shore, I looked over the edge into the water and saw a gray, bloated baby no more than a year old who had died recently but was too young to cremate. I came to understand that when that happens, families tie the baby to rocks and sink them in the Ganges. But sometimes the ropes break loose and the child floats up to the surface.

I couldn't sit in the place where Buddha had received enlightenment without being enlightened by sitting with a group of orphaned boys near lotus flowers. The mixture there of chanting Buddhists and the melody of the music combined with the cries of hungry children and sick adults certainly wasn't what I'd expected, but it was what I needed.

I went to ancient mosques, listened to the beautiful call to prayer, and watched as the sun had just risen and bounced beautifully off the stone walls. All the while, I watched thin and frail children attempt to smile through hungry mouths. Children who went to bed hungry and cold and awoke with little hope that their condition would change.

One of the hardest things about seeing and feeling all this was that since I was traveling alone, I had no one to share the impact with in the evening. No one to talk through what it all meant. There were times when I felt totally alone and did not want to get out of bed in the morning. I would have given anything in those moments to have some companionship, but I think that within me I knew I had to do this by myself. I had to prove to myself that I could do this. It was my own Mount Everest but without the support of a team or a Sherpa. (I did vow that if I ever came back, I wouldn't do it alone. Once was enough without a companion.)

So I saw all these sacred sites. I took this pilgrimage to visit these sacred places, and I came away with an experience I had not been expecting, an experience more powerful than any building or stone. In order to experience the holy in this world, to see places where we believe God has touched or where great spiritual beings have walked, we have to experience how a huge part of humanity lives and tries to survive.

As I stood later in this trip on the shores of the Sea of Galilee near the spot that Jesus is said to have given the Sermon on the Mount, his words rang truer than they have ever rung:

"Blessed are the poor in spirit, for theirs is the kingdom of heaven. Blessed are those who mourn, for they will be comforted. Blessed are the meek, for they will inherit the earth. Blessed are those who hunger and thirst after righteousness, for they will be filled. Blessed are the merciful, for they shall be shown mercy. Blessed are the pure in heart, for they will see God. Blessed are the peacemakers, for they will be called sons of God. Blessed are those who are persecuted, for theirs is the kingdom of heaven."

This pilgrimage I undertook in earnest a few years ago, to go to many of the main places of interest of the five dominant spiritual faiths, had started with great enjoyment and excitement. Though the trip was just simple (me and a backpack), I was feeling the joy of life in foreign countries and the vibrancy of the local people. They might at first be distant in their approach to me, but I was making great progress in my trek.

I had gone to India to sit by the Ganges River. I felt the faith of Hindus, Buddhists, and Muslims in many historic spots where great leaders had received enlightenment. I traveled across the border into Nepal to walk through the birthplace of Buddha, but my trip now needed to turn north and west to Turkey. This would require a plane flight, but first I had to take a train across part of India to return to Delhi so I could catch the plane to Istanbul.

In order to really appreciate the culture of the land, I booked myself in the regular-folks section of the train to Delhi. In India not only are there multiple classes of folks in society (or what they call the caste system), but the trains and much of the rest of the public transportation reflect this class system. On the train, I traveled with the "people"; my section featured uncomfortable seats, unbelievable overcrowding, and interaction at a noisy and way-too-intimate level.

I had been warned by others who had traveled in India to book the best accommodations on trains, because there is much theft and sickness in the other sections. I ignored this advice, because I felt that if I was truly doing a pilgrimage in a foreign land to sacred places, I needed to do it in a way that anyone could experience—not just in the way money and means would allow. If uncomfortable was normal, then I would be uncomfortable.

On the train ride, I was pushed, shoved, and treated in a way that showed me that no one was special. I was okay with all that. When the ride was finished, I realized that nothing had been stolen. I hadn't been physically accosted (I truly was safe and sound). There was just one thing that troubled me: Sitting near me was a very sick man who kept coughing and sneezing. He seemed very ill. This went on for nearly the whole train ride. I thought to myself, I hope I don't get sick. But my ego told me I was healthy, and I was sure I would be okay.

I spent the night in a hotel in Delhi and woke up early the next day to catch the plane to Istanbul. I was feeling run-down and under the weather, but I thought it was from all the days of travel I had under my belt. I could rest and sleep on the long plane ride to Turkey. When I got through security in the Delhi airport (which, by the way, doesn't make you feel all that secure, since the mass of people seem to move through with little rhyme or reason) and took my seat on the plane, I was feeling really sick.

I covered myself with a blanket, drank a lot of water, and fell asleep. After a couple of hours of flying, I woke up to chills and sweating, and I could tell I had a fever. Either from that sick man on the train or somewhere else in the previous day or two, I had caught a pretty bad infection.

My pride had gotten the better of me when I ignored the good advice of experienced travelers and did it my way.

When I walked off the plane in Istanbul and retrieved my oversized backpack at baggage claim, I knew I had a full-blown fever. I was dragging big time and could barely pick myself up to get into a cab. I knew I would need a doctor. In the airport and in the cab to a hotel in the old city of Istanbul, I noticed how much more modern this part of Turkey was compared with India (I had expected them to be comparable). Turkey is such an interesting place, because it is one of the few spots where West meets East all in the same country.

And the history of Turkey is a fascinating study. The country has been involved in so many key points in the journey of the world, with its epic struggles, its international importance, and its cauldron of many different faiths. Turkey is now a secular Muslim country and is home to many ancient sites of both Islam and Christianity. That was what I hoped to see and experience. But first, I had to get to the hotel and find some way to get medical care.

I had a problem: It was a Saturday. No clinics or doctor's offices were open until Monday, according to the man checking me in at my hotel. The only thing he could suggest—and he knew I was pretty sick, since I was sweating and had lost all the color in my face—was a Muslim hospital not far away.

I hesitated for a moment out of fear. I thought, "Here

I am in a foreign land, and I have just recently finished working for President George Bush, whom many Muslims see as the enemy." I decided I had no choice. The hotel folks said they could have Abdullah, a young driver with a car who worked with the hotel, take me. I worked up the energy to say, "Great."

I left my backpack with the man at the front desk and walked outside to find Abdullah standing nearby. The hotel clerk spoke to him in Turkish, telling him I needed to go to the hospital. Abdullah was a very young man, probably no more than twenty-two, with a grim disposition. He agreed to take me.

We got in the car. A short ride later, he pulled up to the Muslim hospital and dropped me off. Abdullah gave me a card with a phone number on it and, in very broken English, said to call him when I needed a ride back to the hotel. Feeling totally abandoned and alone, I was cursing myself for having come on this trip at all. I had no idea what I was going to do. I walked into the Muslim hospital, feeling sick and forlorn.

And this is where things got even worse. No one I could find at the hospital spoke English other than a few words. They knew right away that I was an American by my voice and probably my attitude, even though I was wearing beaten-up clothes, beads around my neck that I had picked up in India and Nepal, and a pretty thick beard.

I attempted to talk to the nurses. They could tell I was

sick, but they didn't exactly know what to do. They got the doctor who was on duty. He also spoke little English. They did a workup on me, taking blood (trust me, in my mind I questioned the cleanliness of everything), my temperature, and other vital signs. I could see the worried look on the doctor's face when the nurse showed him my temperature was 104.3 Fahrenheit. I just wanted to ask him if there were some way I could fly back to Austin and be done with this whole thing.

The doctor determined that I had a pretty bad upper respiratory infection, and I probably was walking around with pneumonia. He gave me one dose of an antibiotic and, in halted English, said I had to fill the prescription as soon as possible, or I would get even sicker. I thought to myself, "How am I going to fill a prescription on a Saturday or a Sunday in this foreign place?" I called Abdullah to pick me up. I decided that if I were going to die (we all get overly dramatic in times like this), I would rather do it in a bed at the hotel than anywhere else.

I got back to the hotel and, with Abdullah standing near me, tried to explain to the clerk that I needed to fill the prescription. The clerk said he didn't know of any pharmacies open; he told me I probably couldn't get it filled until Monday. Just shoot me now, Lord! Abdullah asked me to hand him the prescription; he said he would see what he could do. I went to my room and lay down to rest.

A few hours later, around ten thirty p.m., someone

knocked on my hotel door. I had been asleep for a time and was feeling slightly better from the initial dose of medicine the doctor had provided. I opened the door, and standing there with a paper bag was Abdullah. In the bag was the prescription that he had gotten filled. I was shocked. How had he done it?

In a halting mix of English and Turkish, he explained that one of his relatives had a friend who was a pharmacist. His relative persuaded the pharmacist to leave his home, go into the pharmacy, and fill my prescription. Wow, I didn't know what to say except, "Thank you so much, and how much do I owe you?"

He said, "You owe me nothing. You were sick, and we wanted to help."

My trip, which had started from a dream with such high hopes and enthusiasm to see sacred spots and which had become a disaster in my mind that day, took a huge turn again. A Muslim young man with little money helped this American guy who was a stranger to him and his country. He did it without asking for anything in return. The sick old man on the train in India had given me something that enabled me to experience not a sacred place but a sacred moment. One I will never forget.

So many days in my life, I have been looking for that "big" thing. I am always searching for the answers, even to the broadest reaches of the world. I discovered in this extraordinary moment what I probably had missed so many times. Abdullah probably didn't realize how much this moment deeply affected me and landed in my heart. He was just doing it because that's what he does. Because he saw someone in need and wanted to help.

His faith was Islam, but he was probably one of the most "Christian" people I have ever met. Over the next days, I got better physically and continued on my trip, but this moment stayed with me. How many judgments had I made about faiths and people that I didn't know, how many fears and rationalizations had I embraced because I thought I knew the truth? A new way for the world involves first seeing the good in others as opposed to fearing the bad. This is the new way that many of us are dreaming about for our country and for ourselves.

I have a dream that as Americans we can restore the conversation about faith and patriotism to a holistic place, away from those who use it to divide and judge. I have a dream that there is a better way of relating to one another, a better way for bridging divides, overcoming our politics, and finding integrity in leadership for our country. A new way grounded in faith, hope, and love. A way we are hungry for in this troubled time in America.

INTRODUCTION

We are in a crucial moment. America is at a crossroads. And so is each of us.

We are in a time of tremendous disruption, frustration, anxiety, and confusion. There is ongoing civil discord and divisiveness. We feel disconnected from our own hearts, from one another, and from the values that leaders have spoken and written about for thousands of years. Institutions—financial, economic, political, governmental—are crumbling around us.

We have simultaneously lost faith in nearly every institution that in the past bound us together and helped lead us. Many of us feel like orphans, in search of both community and a new brand of leadership. We know in our hearts that there has to be leadership out there based in integrity, but we keep coming up empty.

We just completed one of the most divisive and unprecedented presidential elections in history. An election for the first time decided between two candidates and two parties that were both distrusted and disliked by a majority of citizens. An election where the losing candidate won a popular-vote victory and the winning candidate won a very close Electoral College decision.

On Election Day, many folks who voted for Donald Trump were angry and frustrated at our current system. They wanted profound change but were very concerned about Trump's manner, temperament, and competence. Many voters wanted change—but to go backward. They were voting as a response to too much change in America in their lives. Most voters desired independent, commonsense leadership but were forced by our broken binary system to pick between two unsatisfactory options. They had to pick between an untrusted outsider versus an untrusted insider. With great trepidation, many went with the outsider. This split-decision electoral result has served only to augment the disruption, angst, and disgust with our current system.

It isn't just in politics that we feel this change. Technological and communication innovation has quickly altered the landscape for leaders at every level forever. CEOs are grappling with more diverse workplaces. Beyond our advancements, the country doesn't even look like how it looked demographically just a few decades ago. We seem more divided than ever before, with Republican versus

Democrat, young versus old, racial divisions, religious divisions, economic divisions, and gender divisions.

Folks who want a restoration of what was and a return to how things used to be are fighting with folks who want to continue on a transformative way into a new world. The people who are looking in the rearview mirror fear change, so they want to move backward. Restoration versus transformation. There is no going back, only moving forward, but in this turbulent world—how?

Profound change is here, and more is coming. We all wonder if we can keep it together as individuals and as a country (and, some would say, as a world). We hunger for more than just surviving through it. We would like to thrive in this wave of change, but we just don't know the way or who can help us. And as we look for leaders to help us along the journey, it seems we keep coming up empty. We search for leadership that is rooted in some deep American values that will reassure us and inspire us, but we are open to a path that may not always be traditional. We are disheartened that many of our leaders are stuck in the conflicts of the past.

This new way forward for ourselves and for our country needs to be based not only in values we have always cherished but also in a new model of how we live and relate to one another. We need new models of what it means to be a leader in our politics, in our businesses, and in our own lives. We are searching for leadership for our country and for every aspect of our lives. We feel both a poverty of leadership and a poverty of the soul.

I am a big believer in cycles of human history. These cycles are especially clear and definitive in the United States. The authors of the seminal cycles of development, William Strauss and Neil Howe, have written much about this in their book *The Fourth Turning*. Every seventy-five or eighty years, they write, this country goes through a series of climactic events, when we experience incredible change and disruption.

Think back to where we were about eighty years ago: We were in midst of the Great Depression, and World War II was on the horizon. New media was growing with radio, television, and movies. Change was occurring in our economics, our business models, our community organizations, the way we communicated with one another, and the way leaders communicated with us.

Think about where we were eighty years before the Depression and World War II: We were in a Civil War, and our country was moving from an agriculture-based economy to an industry-based one. Tremendous change and disruption was occurring in all facets of American life. Not only were we at war with one another as a country, we were also at war with traditional institutional models. We didn't know where to turn in our communities for safety and security.

Eighty years before the Civil War, we were in the midst

of the American Revolution and the establishment of one of the first modern constitutional democracies. We were breaking free from an old model of leadership, trying to establish our own form of governing, which was designed for the benefit of all but without the benefit of a new model to follow. We were leading in the midst of change without a clear example of how this would all work in a new constitutional democracy. We were throwing off an old institution of monarchy and entering into a new path of discovery.

In each of these times in America's past, leaders emerged who were able to bridge the divides. Leaders who seemed to be able to hold competing values simultaneously and who could make decisions in that uncomfortable space many would consider a paradox. George Washington, Abraham Lincoln, and Franklin Roosevelt, while imperfect human beings with many contradictions, were able to lead in a way that provided some stability and security during a time of disruption.

I would add Sam Houston of Texas to the group as well. He was the last independent candidate to win state-wide in the Lone Star State. Although he owned slaves, he was against secession during the lead-up to the Civil War. His principled stand caused him to lose the office of both United States senator and governor in the short term, but in the long term, he became a hero.

Today we have as much economic change as at any

point in our history, and we see after the tragedy of 9/11 that globally we are in a new era of incredible insecurity. The economic and security disruption is immense. Our old models seem to be breaking down around us, and we don't know where to turn. Every single societal institution seems to be crumbling and disintegrating. We have lost faith and trust in what seems like all bonding institutions simultaneously. We don't trust our economic and corporate institutions, our political institutions, the old models of the sexes, our media institutions, and many of our faith structures.

We used to regard all of these institutions as paternalistic and acting in our best interests. No more. After numerous scandals and misbehavior by those in power, Americans have reset their view of, for example, big business. Corporations today are seen as merely profit-motivated, and workers seem to be expendable in a tactical strategy to improve financial value. Governmental actions are viewed as inept, especially at the federal level, and many Americans eye them with disdain.

Our politics have become so partisan that it seems each side is interested only in winning an election, not in advancing the public cause. Those in power have forgotten that country should be put ahead of party. Our news media models have become so fragmented and driven by a partisan agenda that we don't know where to turn for information we can trust. Each side accuses the other of promulgating fake news. We have lost the ability to share a common set of facts, a situation that is disastrous for our republic.

We have even lost faith in our sports structures, which used to be one avenue of binding us together. I have moved around the country over the years and am now settled in Austin, Texas. Because I was born in Detroit, the Detroit teams have still kept my allegiances. I have always been a Tigers fan, a Red Wings fan, a Pistons fan, and a long-suffering Lions fan. But the conversation has changed; each of us is now struggling with trust even in sports.

While reading the paper one day not long ago, I observed that we have a hard time trusting the records in baseball because of drugs. At times, we watch the NFL leadership put profit over the health of their players. We see players and referees betting on their own games in baseball and the NBA. And then there is the Tour de France, which has become a tragic joke, where we don't even know the "winners" anymore.

For many folks today, this is all too much. They retreat into the safe enclaves of their homes, throw up their hands, and conclude that nothing can be done. There is just too much change and so many ongoing failures that we have no idea how to fix them or where to turn. We are frustrated, apathetic, and becoming cynical. We assign the good life to yesterday and regard the future as bleak. Or we grasp too tightly to old models or ways that no longer fit the dynamics of today. We put on the jersey of Democrat or Republican and view everything through a partisan lens, and as a result, the truth is lost. America has broken down into tribes that merely fight one another.

Today we have access to tons of data and other information because of technology, but we use it to support tribal positions. We seem to have more knowledge and less wisdom. We gather information that only confirms what we already believe, and we ignore news or information that makes us uncomfortable. Our confirmation bias only divides us more, because opinions turn into "facts" when we seek only confirming information. And you can't reach consensus if everyone is operating from their own "fact" set. Yes, without a common set of facts, we have no chance of getting to the common good, which is fundamentally the basis for our system of government.

We choose between detaching too much from all that matters and concluding that everything is relative, on the one hand, and holding on too tightly to an old institution that is worn out, on the other hand. Either we become apathetic just trying to make it through the day watching some reality TV show to distract us from the pain we feel, or we think someone else is responsible for fixing the ills of the world. We work for or elect a president or new members of Congress, hoping they will fix all that is wrong. Then, when nothing changes, we are gravely disappointed and retreat more into the silos of our lives.

Because of this, it is easy to become negative, bitter, scared, and disheartened. But I believe with profound disruption comes the opportunity for needed change. It is when one is most hungry that we go out and find sustenance. It is when our pain is at its height that we are motivated to fix it.

We are in a time of tremendous hunger and pain. It is in this moment when we diligently look for a new way—as individuals and as the world in general. We all see the unbelievable poverty around us, and we know this needs to be addressed. But the greatest poverty that exists in ourselves, our communities, and our country today is poverty of the soul, which breeds poverty of leadership.

This poverty of the soul, where we are searching for meaning, deeper connections, and grounded values, affects people at the richest levels of our society as well as those with the fewest resources. The wounds in our hearts and souls are as grievous in the wealthiest communities as they are in the poorest (joy and happiness are not determined by possessions). This lack of real leadership exists not only in the broad circles of the country but also in the small, intimate circles of our individual lives.

Many folks have lost the optimistic joy of living; they have just settled for surviving in either silent or loud deprivation. We know that there should be more (those quiet voices inside us tell us this)—more meaning, more happiness, more connection—but we struggle for how to get there or what the solution is to our own pain or the country's. We are more connected but less in touch. We search for a new brand of leadership, but we seem to have difficulty discovering it.

We each are seeking a new way forward. A new brand of leadership that helps us resolve these conflicting values and points a way forward for us, for our institutions, and for the country as a whole. Leadership that puts country over party, community over profit, the Constitution over personal power, and the broad over the narrow. And as citizens, we are also going to have to behave at the ballot box in a country-over-party manner—breaking old, ingrained partisan habits.

Willoughby, a good-hearted, lost, and somewhat dim-witted hound, starred in a 1940 Warner Brothers cartoon titled *Of Fox and Hounds* alongside George, a sly and mischievous fox. Willoughby's job was to catch the fox, but George would dress up not very convincingly as a dog and misdirect Willoughby, usually into some tragedy, such as going over a cliff. Willoughby would approach George and say repeatedly, "Which way did he go, George? Which way did he go?" not suspecting that the fulfillment of his mission was standing right in front of him. I discovered the same thing about myself as I searched for a new leadership model.

A little less than a decade ago, in the midst of tremendous transition in my own life, I decided to preoccupy myself in a new business endeavor. I had been an entrepreneur my whole life, progressing from a *Detroit News* paper route as a youngster, to neighborhood lawn work, to a painting company in college in St. Louis, to numerous political campaigns. I had even opened a coffee shop with one of my sisters in a small town in central Texas called Burro, hoping to create a sense of community and have some fun. (Maybe I was using that particular business venture as a distraction from what I really needed to focus on in my personal life, but it seemed to be in my comfort zone. Beware when you do stuff that seems to be in your comfort zone.) Anyway, cofounding what became a well-known international public affairs company seemed the natural thing to do.

The startup business concept was a "branding and strategy" venture based in Austin, where I live. It would involve giving advice and counsel to other large companies, associations, and foundations. Some old friends and partners, who had separate companies and with whom I had worked in politics from both sides of the aisle, would come together under one umbrella business to provide a hoped-for profitable professional career. We each had confidence that this would be successful and that we could have fun together, but one thing was missing. We needed a name.

Each of us involved struggled with coming up with a company name. We bounced around many ideas and words, but none seemed to fit or strike us as creative enough.

Then one day, I had a thought or just a hunch. I had no idea where it came from, but over the years, I have learned to pay attention to these quiet voices within myself. What about trying to tie something old with something new?

I had taken Latin in high school and college, and I loved the language; it has the feel of antiquity and is a language of knowledge and insight. I played with some words and finally settled on *Vianova*, which roughly translates into "new way." The other partners thought it was awesome, and off we went. But we first had to research who might have the domain name already (a challenge of the modern era). And that is where the story took a funny turn.

Initially, we discovered that the name Vianova was taken. Also, *nova* means "don't go" in Spanish (the Chevy Nova had famously underperformed in South America), so this seemed like a poor root from which to build our brands. So, we quickly switched gears to Vianovo, which is a combination of the feminine and masculine genders in Latin. That fact should have been sending me some signals from the universe that this name might have had more import than just about a company. Already here was the need to resolve seemingly conflicting values.

This being a twenty-first-century founding and our living in a world that is simultaneously large and very interconnected, it turns out that the domain was already owned by someone in St. Petersburg, Russia. We discovered that we could buy it from the fellow there for $940. We made the deal, and now we had a name and a company. Slowly we built it. It still strikes me as ironic and hilarious that people who worked in United States politics came up with a Latin-named business, mis-combined the feminine and the masculine, and purchased the domain name from someone in the former Soviet Union. It is truly a global world.

The business has done very well. Our revenues have grown each year, and our partners and employees make a good living, so they can raise their families in communities they love. But at some point a few years ago, I became less enamored with giving advice to corporate, foundation, or large-association clients. It didn't strike me as something that made me passionate or enthusiastic, and I felt I wanted more meaning in my life. A few years ago, I left this company to explore other ways I might add value to the conversations in leadership circles, and this book is one such attempt.

As I have contemplated my life ahead, I have begun more and more to ask deeper questions and seek answers. Today as I reflect on that name of Vianovo, I realize that this story of starting a company has much broader and deeper import. Like the Warner Brothers hound Willoughby, I kept getting redirected and making many wrong turns, because I couldn't clearly see that my real job or mission was standing right in front of me.

Vianovo wasn't really about starting a business; it was

much more about finding a new way forward, not only for myself as a leader but possibly for our country. I guess I understood intuitively and subconsciously that my own story needed a new way, and with tremendous disruption and change going on simultaneously within me and around all of us, so does our world. I finally looked through the disguises and saw George the fox.

This new way forward needed to be rooted not only in some deep values of old but also in a new model for how we live and relate to one another in politics, relationships, economic structures, and religion or spirituality. I have come to believe that what is best for the country has to start with a model and practice that works and is best for the individual. We can't change the world and make it a better, more loving place until we change ourselves.

This new way forward needs to be based on an entrepreneurial model. A model based on integrity first and foremost, as well as innovation, imagination, and ingenuity. We forget that our founding fathers and mothers of this great country were the ultimate entrepreneurs. They began the ultimate startup—a country. Though these were men of great means and position and rank, they risked all of it to create institutions that worked on behalf of all Americans. They put life, liberty, and land on the line to begin anew. We must adopt the same spirit today in our leadership models.

In the United States and around the world, entrepreneurs

in both the business and nonprofit sectors are rising up in a major way in community after community. They are disrupting old broken systems with innovative solutions to chronic problems—high-tech engagement involving products and services, creating new neighborhood communities, using the law for change, or reimagining philanthropy. This goes on while our politics and governance seem lost in a desert of imagination, where we have forsaken the great independence we so proudly celebrate on the anniversary of the Declaration of Independence. As the last line of that Declaration says: "We mutually pledge to each other our Lives, our Fortunes, and our Sacred Honor."

It is time that we change this. We need more entrepreneurs and fewer opportunists. We need a political and governing model that supports creativity and imaginative ways to confront the problems that face us in the future. Without imagination, we lose hope, and without hope we no longer see that change is possible. We need to find a new way.

A big first step in finding a new way of leading is to pay attention as best we can to the whispering voices within our hearts to what might be standing right in front of us. Those voices start out so weak that many times we can't hear them at all. We rush around with so much activity and noise in our lives that we can't hear the quiet calling within our own bodies. It is like the ping of the black box of a downed airplane. Lying deep in the ocean, it sends a faint signal to give us a way to the truth. The voices are heard but are so low that they are drowned out by all the louder voices in our heads from parents, siblings, and friends, to coworkers or even strangers. The voices that say, "That is ridiculous." "Don't do that." "You shouldn't do this." "That won't work."

Or we search on the surface, looking for remnants of our lives, afraid to dive deep and discover the truth lying at the bottom of the ocean of our souls. It is these quiet voices in the recesses of our being that ultimately lead us to the truth and to our purpose in life. They give us the answers we are searching for. Even though there is tremendous pressure and fear at the depths of the search, it is there that we find meaning and a new way. I thought Vianovo was about doing business, but it really was about my own business and that of the country.

Each of us has an important story about how we piece this together. But the solution begins with our own lives, our own world, and our own relationships. Unfortunately, looking for the next big thing distracts us from the real change that can happen. We tend to think that if we do our civic duty or our charitable duty and vest someone else with our power to make the change happen (whether it be in politics or in giving money to a charity), then we did what we could.

In that manner, when we give our power away, we end up more bitter when nothing seems to change. We project that the leaders are out there somewhere, or that it is someone else's job to be a leader, when we need to realize that each of us is called for leadership in some way.

What is this new way of leadership that provides each of us some model of living and leading in life? What type of leaders need to emerge to create positive impact in our communities and country? What is the brand of American leadership we demand? What will the next president need to do to inspire our country? What will show us the light on the path ahead through the unknown, which will help us pick leaders who can maneuver through all this disruption and confusion? What will help us put country over party? Fundamentally, the answer is that we must embrace the paradox of conflicting values, and it is in the uncomfortable balance of those competing pulls where we can find the new way to lead.

That is the story of America.

And that is fundamentally what each of our own stories is.

CHAPTER ONE

LIVING OUR CONTRADICTIONS

America started with a story, one based on the dreams of people who wanted a new way to live as a country. We each have our own story, wrapped in the story of our country. We all share our stories with one another, our friends, and our family. Stories are the way we learn about life: from fables we learned as a child, to the stories about our ancestors, to the history and literature we read in school, to movies and television, and to the story of our lives. And every great story, with all its valuable lessons, is filled with contradictions and paradox.

How do we really grow and learn throughout life? How do our story and our values fit in with our country's? This question confronts all of us all the time. How wisely we answer it determines how well we live.

Is the important information we impart to one another a set of facts, historical points, evidence of what works or what doesn't work, or key news? To me, the way we become the people we are meant to be is by listening to and telling stories, especially personal stories that come from a place of either pain, or joy, or craziness.

Think about it: If someone tells us what we should do by merely giving us some trite slogan or moralistic saying, we usually nod our heads, listen as intently as we can, and try to understand it or make it part of ourselves. But it doesn't sink in unless it is attached to a story, and that story must feel real to us. It needs to be one in which we understand the journey of the characters in that story.

The story can be fiction or nonfiction, filled with many folks or just with one person. Stories that touch us must engage our hearts long before they engage our heads. Logical information makes us do the instinctual head nod. Heartfelt information or gut-level communication makes us change or evolve into better people.

Throughout my career in politics, business, and broadcasting, I've learned the power of a narrative. Voters, clients, and viewers respond to a compelling story, not a simple sound bite. They are interested not just in what you are saying but who you are, where you've been, and what you've learned.

Stories touch us. The good stories make us laugh,

cry, think, question, and celebrate. The best messages are wrapped up in stories, whether you hear them in a sermon at church, from a candidate running for office, or when leaning over a backyard fence. Stories move us and open our whole wide world.

The ancient Greeks told stories to one another. These stories became the myths we read in school. Romans of old told stories that have become movies or quotes in our modern books or that are plastered on our walls. Native Americans sat around campfires and told one another stories, which became part of the coming of age, when youth entered manhood or womanhood. Jesus told stories (parables) and conveyed truths and a way of life through the telling.

Nearly every great leader in history told stories so we could learn, think, and discover. Leaders tell stories to bring people in and create a common bond. The best presidents have told stories and have connected with us. Each of us tells stories for the same reasons.

But we don't just read stories: we live them. Each one of us every day is taking part in a story. As we walk through life, it is important that we discover our own story and live that story as authentically and bravely as possible. Then, we must tell that story to someone or many other someones. The people we love want to hear our story, because it is the only way we know one another, can connect with one another, and understand one another and ourselves.

Our ability to live our own story, feel it, know it, and then tell it is one of the most important parts of our way in the world. This self-knowledge enables us to discover things we need to know about ourselves and others. Without a story or a vision, we are lost and ungrounded. We flounder and search until we find a story to settle into, and then we know our way.

It is when we are confused about our own story, forget our story, feel so bad about our story, judge ourselves and then never tell it, that we create confusion and anxiety in our own lives. It takes a brave person to dig deep, discover their own story, and then tell it to another. We really can't love or be loved if we don't know our own story and tell it to someone.

Sometimes in telling our story to someone else, we discover a broken trust or a judgment. That doesn't make our story wrong; it just means we told it to the wrong person. Or maybe even in their judgment, they learned something from our story. Nonetheless, this experience teaches us we can't trust everyone with our most intimate stories.

It is in this discovery of our stories—with all our hopes and dreams, failings and fun, mistakes and merriment, achievements and heartbreaks—that we give to ourselves, others, and ultimately the world what is so desperately needed. A life that is genuine and filled with glimpses of how we can be happy or fulfilled and help one another is the ultimate goal. In this journey, we discover that life isn't about consistency, but about a flow in the paradoxical moments.

Telling a story and listening to someone else's story is really one of the greatest services we can give to the world. If we want to be of service, sharing stories is one of the most profound ways to do that. Our stories shine a light on truths that we all need to hear and see. Your story matters as much as mine or that of any famous person or celebrity who tells their story. To matter and have an impact, the book of your life doesn't have to be a bestseller.

One thing I have learned about stories and about life is that the path to a life fulfilled with passion and purpose lies in how we live the story that is in our journals, in our diaries, in the margins of a book, or in the deep recesses of our hearts and minds. We write down in secret or in private our hopes, our dreams, and how we want to live, but then, sadly, we live a completely different life in practice. The stories we want to live and tell exist like a canyon between what we are doing on a day-to-day basis and what we dream of or hope to be doing.

Bridging this canyon requires the strength and courage it takes for us to live the life that is in our journals, including our work, our families, our relationships, our politics, and our business practices. Filling that canyon causes major disruption in our lives and the lives of others. The fulfillment of our story may need to include our quitting a job, standing up for ourselves, ending a relationship, quitting a political party, or spending time with our children that we missed along the way. Closing a chapter will likely involve judgments from others, criticism from many, and a thousand misunderstandings. People will think we are lost when we are actually trying to find our way.

As I learned to be open and to embrace the paradox, much of how I came to this leadership model was informed by people and events in my life. Along the way, I learned a few things that struck me as important about leadership. Those lessons gave me a new way of leading and living, as well as some insight into a new way for our country.

At the end of 1988, I had just started a company (Public Strategies Inc.) with another partner. We were trying to build up a practice of public affairs clients. The company wasn't designed to do political consulting, but the opportunity to work on Texas State Comptroller Bob Bullock's campaign for lieutenant governor seemed exciting and could have a big impact in Texas. The office of lieutenant governor in Texas is very powerful, with leadership over committee assignments, legislation, and appointments. In fact, many see this office of lieutenant governor as more powerful than that of the governor of Texas. This model had been set up in Texas so that too much power would not be vested in a single chief executive.

Being the strategist in Comptroller Bullock's campaign was quite a dramatic change from the previous campaign I had worked on in Texas, which was on behalf of US

Senator Lloyd Bentsen. That race had started out with my helping set up the campaign for Senator Bentsen running for reelection as a senator, but I ended up working on the joint ticket in Texas after Bentsen was picked by Governor Michael Dukakis as the vice presidential nominee in the 1988 campaign. In Texas there is something called the "LBJ law," passed when LBJ ran as vice president in 1960, allowing a politician to run for two offices at once. It seems that only in Texas, the only state to be an independent country before it became part of the United States, can we create our own rules.

From Bentsen to Bullock—talk about two Texas legends cut from totally different cloth.

Bentsen was very smart, a little cool, and a bit patrician. Maybe more than a bit—he definitely was patrician. He came from a prominent wealthy family in south Texas, and he carried himself with a strong, quiet demeanor. He hardly swore at all, talked in a slow manner, and often didn't say much. He wasn't one for the party circuit, and he seemed to only drink socially. He was always dressed perfectly, with starched shirts and not a stitch out of place. Bullock on the other hand? Not so much.

Bullock was really the old-style Texas politician. He was much more akin to the Lyndon Baines Johnson type of pol. He had a swagger and toughness and a little "screw the rules" style, mixed with a big heart. Bullock lived large, talked big, and had big dreams for the state. And boy, could he swear and talk a blue streak! He had been married five times (twice to the same woman), was a heavy drinker in his day (he had sworn off all liquor and had been in Alcoholics Anonymous for years before he died), and smoked as if there were no tomorrow.

One time when I went hunting with him on a cold day, Bullock said he had given up smoking and was wearing nicotine patches. I was sitting with my rifle in the bed of the truck and watched him through the window light up a cigarette. He just looked back at me and smiled. The only thing I could think of was what was I going to do when he had a nicotine-induced heart attack? Bullock had what can best be described as a volatile temper as well as a wry sense of humor. He never directed that temper at me (though he did at many others), but his humor was always a weapon.

Even after his four divorces, he still believed in marriage. I have often said that anyone who gets married multiple times is the ultimate optimist, so he was an incredible optimist. He wasn't always faithful in his relationships, but he was always loyal to his friends, oftentimes to a fault. He would do anything for someone he loved or cared about. He remembered Christmas, birthdays, and anniversaries for me and all my kids until the day he died.

I remember when I was going through my first divorce. I was talking to him, given his own history, about my situation. The first thing Bullock said as I sat in his office at the Texas state capitol, trying to get some advice, was, "I don't believe in divorce." Really? After four marriages?

He talked about the effect divorce has on the couple, and on their kids, and how if he had to do it all over again, he would have been much more thoughtful.

His advice to me as I went through my separation and divorce was to honor what I had shared with my spouse and treat her well in the process. Don't let it become bitter, he said, and don't use the kids in the process as a pawn. He even went so far as to assist the mother of my three boys, the woman I was divorcing, in finding work at the state capitol, to make sure she would be financially okay in the aftermath. All good advice and actions, which I have tried to abide by as best I could in the years since.

He was chock-full of stories and character. I remember sitting down for one of my first campaign meetings with him and the rest of his advisers. As the campaign strategist, I was sitting across from Mr. Bullock (I always called him that—never Bob, even though we had become good friends) at a round table in an old two-story house in West Austin, going over poll numbers. I had my head bent down over the numbers, trying to make sense of them.

He stopped me and said, "You are going bald."

I said, "I know, Mr. Bullock," and tried to get back to the numbers and strategy.

Later on he said again, "Matthew, you are going bald!"

I again said I knew; then I looked him in the eye and said, "Okay. And so?"

He then asked me, "Do you know how to cure that?" I said no.

He then said with a totally straight face in front of everyone, "You've got to get a virgin to pee on your head." I said, "Oh really!" and tried not to laugh.

He then added, "But make sure she's a virgin. Otherwise, you will get pinkeye." So much for all the points I was trying to make at the strategy meeting.

And then he wanted to get back to the seriousness of the meeting and the campaign strategy. I shook my head and went on, laughing to myself about him. He has been gone more than fifteen years, but I still remember all his tales as though they were yesterday.

Bullock asked me one day if I had ever been so drunk that I shot my washing machine. I shook my head and was able to confidently say, "No." He then proceeded to tell me that one night he came home totally sloshed on booze after downing at least a fifth of something. He looked at his wall, with all the stuffed animal heads that he had hunted and mounted. He thought they were coming to life, so he loaded his rifle and started shooting them. After four or five shots from his gun, he then sobered up a bit and decided to do laundry. He put clothes in the washer, turned it on, and went to sleep on the couch. He woke to water all over the floor. He went to the washer and found a bullet hole. Nope, I've never been so drunk that I shot the washer.

He suffered from lung cancer and had a lung removed a while before he died. Still, he continued to chain-smoke off and on, sometimes embracing quitting and sometimes embracing the cigarettes. He actually helped fund more cancer research in Texas than had been funded anytime prior. That's just who he was—a man who embodied so many contradictions.

A lot of folks would shake their heads about Bullock and say they didn't like him or that he was vengeful or that his temper was crazy. All of that is justified to some degree, but he never treated me poorly, and I was never on the bad end of one of his tirades. I have a very fond place in my heart for the man.

He made many mistakes in his life. He lived large. But he also loved large. And he was the kind of friend anyone would want to have. He helped so many people through troubled times, getting them into AA, or hiring someone as a second chance, or giving someone advice when they needed it most. He even helped then-Governor Bush achieve bipartisan support in passing legislation in Texas on education, the economy, and funding for many needs. I have often thought that if Bullock had still been alive when Bush became president, maybe things would have turned out differently.

Bullock even intersected with one of my younger sisters when she moved to Texas. Kelly was the eighth of the eleven of us, and she was struggling with addiction. When

I asked him as a favor, Bullock hired her to work for him to help her out. She seemed to be doing okay and was getting a handle on her life, but one never knows. Kelly began looking backward in her life, and at some point, after being in Austin about a year, she decided to move back to the Detroit area. Things became disruptive, and her story got very complicated and tragic. The next time I saw her, she wasn't able to look back.

I remember gathering on a cold day at a small Catholic church near Flint, Michigan, a few years ago. The words "drugs… overdose… death" kept swirling around in my head. The phrase "she was an addict" was knocking around in there, too, as though it was supposed to define my younger sister Kelly's life. Kelly died suddenly and tragically. She was buried the day before Thanksgiving in near-frozen Michigan dirt, leaving behind three young and beautiful children searching for answers and her family and friends groping for explanations.

Kelly died alone in her month-to-month rental house right as the holidays were starting. She was found sprawled across her bathroom floor, an open bottle of pills nearby and a half-drunk bottle of wine on the kitchen counter. This was an end to a life that had such promising beginnings. She had been a child always so full of tenderness and with a huge heart. She was smart, but also very sensitive. She was a person who loved life, but she was constantly seeking affirmation and acceptance. In a large family such as ours, I fear her sensitivity was battered a bit, and she hadn't received a lot of the affirmation she needed while growing up. We will never really know where it all began.

Kelly, like so many of us, was constantly searching for joy and happiness. She just didn't realize until it was too late that the only way she would find it was by looking within and discovering it inside her. She moved around a bit, went to college briefly in Iowa, and then came to Texas. She seemed to be doing well. As I mentioned, she got a good job working for the state of Texas (through Bullock's help), moved into a funky apartment in Austin, and got herself a dog. She seemed happy on the outside, but something was troubled within.

She decided she would be happier moving back to Michigan. She went back to school in the Detroit area, graduated with honors, met a good guy, and got married. Again, all seemed to be going well externally, but beneath the surface she was struggling. Kelly mistakenly felt her peace and happiness involved moving to a different place or finding a different guy.

Kelly had her three children in pretty quick order and was constantly sending pictures to all of us, showing how adorable they were. We all knew that Kelly drank too much and that she had started taking prescription pills to numb her pain. Numerous times, her husband tried to help, but to no avail. Kelly started acting out more and more. At times, when she wasn't coherent, she even put her children in harm's way. Many of us brothers and sisters tried to come to her aid and give her advice. At best, our efforts were temporary, and nothing seemed to stick. I still ask the question today if there had been more I could have done. Probably we will always be asking the question.

She ended up getting divorced. Her husband couldn't take the dysfunction and dramatic ups and downs that were a constant at that point. He was also worried about the environment their children were being raised in. There were times her kids had to call EMS themselves to help their mom. Kelly floundered from job to job, and she kept moving around to different spots in Michigan. She would see her kids, but not all that often. Every day she seemed to keep trying to live a better life, but her efforts didn't seem to have roots.

People say that you can't help addicts until they really want to help themselves. They say that an addict has to hit bottom before they start climbing up. For some people, the bottom might be a big argument or an arrest for a DWI or spending one night in jail. I guess for my sister, her bottom was much further down. She never seemed to reach it in a way that would cause a permanent shift in her behavior.

After the funeral, there were many things that had to be taken care of. Legal matters, dealing with the police report, and trying to figure out what to do with the few possessions she left behind. For all of those who have to pack up clothes from someone who died suddenly—their books, kitchen supplies, glasses, and plates—it is such a wrenching thing. We decided to give almost all of it away to a Catholic charity in Flint. The city of Flint has been suffering for a good long while after the auto industry declined; the number of homeless has climbed dramatically, and today the city has poisoned drinking water. We thought Kelly's big heart could live on in that community she called home.

At one point when we siblings were packing up her belongings from her rental house to take across town to the needy in our pickup trucks, my older brother Pat leaned into me and said, "Hey, Matt, you know what they found in the pocket of the pajamas she died in? A Christmas list of presents she wanted to buy her kids." Whoa, that just stopped me dead in my tracks. You try to be strong in these instances, but tears spontaneously flowed from my eyes.

In our culture, it's common—even encouraged—to default to the sound bite, the quick headline, or the snap judgment to define one another and explain the world around us. It's a default that I, unfortunately, have done very easily at times in political discussions. It's something I used to be paid to do when I ran campaigns for Republicans as well as Democrats: the quick analysis, the succinct message point. Make it short, make it memorable, and make it stick. We think the simple message is the truth, and the complex or complicated is uncomfortable and won't resonate.

Does this worship of the simple, the brief, and the

consistent get us any closer to the truth? Or does it take us further away from it? Does it give us the leadership we crave, or does it lead us away? Does it help us put country over party?

The food in the refrigerator was still fresh with the lunch meat Kelly was probably going to have the next day and the vegetables she just didn't get to that night. Notes were posted on the refrigerator door to remind her of the things she needed to do, amid pictures her kids had drawn for her at grade school to remind her of the loves in her life.

My sister's place was littered with signs of a more complicated truth than the one obscured by the easy headline. A life that was a bit of a paradox, but not one she could ever resolve. She had twenty-four-hour Alcoholics Anonymous coins lying all over her house, on tables and in dishes. Each of these coins is given out at meetings to mark a day of sobriety, and she attended meetings all the time. She knew it was helpful, and she knew in her head that she wanted to get better; it just didn't gather deep enough roots in her heart.

She had weights in the living room for her workouts. She always wanted to stay in shape and she wanted people to find her attractive. Religious, spiritual, and poetry books were scattered about, with freshly underlined passages on faith, hope, and love. The movie *The Bucket List* was near her DVD player. She had either just watched it or was about to. It's a wonderful film starring Jack Nicholson and

Morgan Freeman about preparing for death and enjoying life in the meantime. About finding what is important in life and not wasting one precious minute of this mystery we call life.

And, of course, the folded Christmas list in her pocket, her notes about what she wanted to give the folks she cared about. A piece of paper that reflected her love of her kids and the hope and joy that comes with giving.

As we walk through life and deal with one another, we need to keep in mind that truth is not in the headline or the pithy, consistent sound bite. Truth is deeper in the heart and soul of each of us. It is in the good intentions that most of us carry with us every day, as we make mistakes along the way. It is found in the incredible paradox of living and leading. Diving down to those depths rather than just snorkeling in the shallows might give us the bends. But it also might tell us a little more about one another and ourselves. It might reveal the power of resolving the paradox in our values and our lives that can give us direction and a way forward as leaders. My sister and Mr. Bullock were symbols of a valuable insight I walked away with.

Bullock was a human metaphor for life. He was a thundering paradox of a man, but somehow, in the end, it all made sense. From Bullock, I learned that we can all make mistakes, but it is how we learn from them and live with them that really tell us the kind of person we are. He never blamed anyone else but himself when things went wrong.

And he never saw himself as a victim. He would just wake up each day and try to live it as big he could. He realized the havoc he had wreaked in his life, but he didn't let it get in the way of doing well for others. Bullock had his demons, but he also had his angels. Just like all of us, he was a mixture of the good and bad jumbled up like a stew that each of us is trying to make sense of.

And that's really a lesson for us all. We each have a whole batch of contradictions that we aren't supposed to erase, but rather embrace. Life isn't the search for consistency, but rather balance. We are responsible for how we weave those contradictions together. We can all do good and bad, and we are all part saint and sinner trying to do the best we can. As I learned from Bullock, my sister, and many others, leading is about finding the balance in the paradox between saint and sinner. It is in that place that we can lead our own lives. It is in that place where broad leadership for our country must necessarily be found.

CHAPTER TWO

PARADOX: ESTABLISHING THE BRAND

In the past twenty-five years, there have been innumerable books written about and speeches given on leadership. These ideas have been pushed by businesspeople, candidates for office, consultants, historians, heads of foundations, wealthy people, sports figures, and a plethora of celebrities. I don't discount any of the knowledge one can gain from reading these books or hearing these speeches. The difficulty comes in practice, because as a leader, you are constantly presented with a series of conflicting value propositions. Nearly every one of these books or speeches is about picking one set of values and making these a disciplined practice throughout one's leadership.

Consistency is a hallmark of nearly every leadership model explored and promulgated in the past couple of generations. Even in campaigns for public office, candidates who aren't consistent on a set of issues or who come across as "nuanced" are attacked for not holding firmly to a set of principled values. I was the chief strategist on the campaign for President George W. Bush's reelection, where we unrelentingly went after former Senator John Kerry for being a flip-flopper.

The contrast was presented as the difference between a strong and principled leader (Bush) versus a weaker, inconsistent leader (Kerry). With this simple dynamic presented to the American people, Bush came out ahead, because Kerry was never able to demonstrate that there is strength in holding a more balanced, or nuanced, position. This didn't get us closer to the truth, unfortunately.

As we move into the unknown years ahead, as we try to navigate a confusing and tumultuous present, the leaders who will achieve success are those who can hold the balance of seemingly opposing ways and values. These leaders must learn to embrace the paradox. Not only will it be the political leaders we pick to lead our country who must be able to stand in the conflict and embrace the paradox, but it will be business leaders, heads of associations, community leaders, and elected officials at all levels. Every one of us, in leading our own lives, must learn to stand tall in the paradox of competing values. This will be the only path to improve not only our individual lives but also the country as a whole.

Webster's defines paradox as "something that is made up of two opposite things and that seems impossible but is actually true or possible." Danny Miller, in his book *Icarus Paradox*, based an analysis of business success or failure on the Greek myth of Icarus. Icarus, who was given wings made of wax by his father, flew too close to the sun. His wings melted, and he fell to the ocean and drowned. Miller pointed out the paradox involving businesses that succeed but then suddenly fail for the same reasons they had succeeded. It is in understanding the importance of paradox in life that we can succeed as leaders and find a president who will lead our country forward.

As we look across the span of interactions and leadership dynamics, we can identify hundreds of paradoxes. There is probably a paradox in nearly every action or reaction we take as we walk through life, each one setting up a decision to be made about who we are or how we are going to present ourselves. This is ultimately what our brands are.

As leaders, and especially for those in politics, the brand of the individual is key. Your brand is what tells voters, consumers, and even people in our own living rooms who we are. It is not just presidents or parties or businesses that have brands—no, each one of us has a brand. We each, in our own leadership circles of our lives, convey in spoken and unspoken ways who we are. This is how we connect with others. Our brands facilitate success or failure in our work, relationships, and connections. Our own brands matter as much as a presidential candidate's brand. Every success begins with a brand.

But there is a paradox in even figuring out how we want to communicate to others who we are. In every campaign I've worked on, I've mined the quarry to get at the soul of the state or country. In every company I've consulted with, I've worked hard to find out the DNA of that particular company. In my broadcasting, I have tried to never have any persona other than my own. Sometimes, I do this very well; other times, I don't.

Having been involved with a lot of different folks and organizations, helping them get elected or otherwise win something or accomplish their goal, I have a pretty good understanding of what it means to communicate a brand. This understanding applies to presidents, large nonprofit foundations in the world, multinational corporations, the NBA, and a bevy of others. I have spent a lot of time focusing on their brands and what values those brands entail. I try to ascertain whether the organization is supporting the brand.

The process of life is discovering what our brands are, and then ensuring that the brands are protected and communicated externally. This may sound a bit sterile and academic, but it is probably one of the most important things we can do to achieve our purpose in the world and to be happy. Defining and communicating your brand is the road to finding your way in life.

And this is where the paradox comes in. Many people confuse their "bio" with their brand. They define themselves by their attributes and roles, some of which they have little or no control over. They think their brand is where they were born; what ethnicity they are; their physical attributes or what they do; whether they are married, have children, and what family they come from; or a hundred other biographical pieces of information.

These elements are all important; they help define who we are, and they impact how we make decisions. They are also indicators of aspects of our brands. But they are *not* our brands. When asked who they are or if they connect with someone, most people, most of the time, relate to their biography. But biography is not brand.

So, what is a brand? Based on my professional experience and my personal reflections, I believe that a brand is our values. Specifically, it's the values that define who we are, what we believe, and how we live. These values often have competing aspects or conflicting decision modes. Your brand could be that you are a compassionate, soulful human being. Or that you are a person who is comfortable much of the time in quiet solitude. That you are gregarious and shine when people are around. That you are competitive and need a daily challenge to motivate yourself. That you are exceedingly tolerant and not judgmental. Or that you are very good at decisions and making reasoned judgments. Your brand is your Code.

There are so many different values that a brand can be. It is not one value that defines our own individual brand but a set of values that come together and make us uniquely who we are. Our brands are the interesting mix of values that we are born with, that life creates in us, and that are highlighted along the way.

This is one of the biggest challenges I have experienced in my professional career. I have seen so many candidates or organizations that never fully understood their brand or the paradox involved in the act of decision making from competing values. As a result, they had a very difficult time succeeding at their goals. More importantly, they didn't understand that maybe their goals or their mission wasn't in sync with their brand.

Even people who are attuned to and observe politics or who cover and comment on presidential campaigns are in error about what matters. Presidential campaigns are not fundamentally about issues or biographies or personalities or the manner of a candidate. Presidential campaigns, like our own lives, are about values and, thus, brands. Your success in the years ahead will be about embracing the paradox of competing values of your brand so you can make decisions from a centered place.

Maybe an individual was raised in a family where running for office was a part of everyone's biography and that then became their goal. But they never took the time to see if running for office matched their real values, not just their bio or their legacy. Maybe they felt more at home writing poetry, or owning a clothing store or a farm—whatever it might have been. Maybe those activities would have been more in sync with their values and should have been their goal instead of politics.

We can discover, understand, and live our brands early in life or late in life. If we are going to be happy and fulfilled, we need to protect those brands and match many aspects of our lives to those brands. Ironically, most of us understand our brands early in life, but then we are pushed to conform to our biography and we lose sight of our brands. Or some event in life twists us or turns us around so that we don't know anymore what our brands are.

The pressures of the world—both small and large—are very strong and are determined to make us conform to either the brands or the biographies of others. They push us to be consistent and predictable. People all around us lay expectations on our shoulders and try to convince us what our brands are or what we should be doing. Others try to tell us that we have to pick one way or the other, and they push us away from embracing the paradox of our values. If we don't have a good sense of our own brands or the strength in our brands, we lose the compass point that should be the main way we navigate in life. We lose the ability to hold the paradox as a decision-making mode, and we lose our brands.

When I was young, I had a very good sense of my own brand. I was carefree, fun-loving, extroverted, optimistic, and very interested in spirituality, and I loved to be the leader in a group. I could maintain the balance of many competing values and embrace the paradox. All of us as children found it natural to be what some would call "inconsistent." We each knew inherently as a child that the truth was in the paradox. This was true for me even at the age of seven or eight.

Along the way, I lost sight of this, or I convinced myself that I was different from the values and traits I just described. I became untethered from my own brand. I began living and acting in life in a way much different from those core values. Like a ship without an anchor, I drifted in the rough winds and wild seas of life. At some point I had become convinced, as did many folks around me personally and professionally, that I was introverted, a little dark, and a good bit pessimistic. In fact, I had a sign on my door at the campaign that quoted Yeats: "The Irish have an abiding sense of tragedy that sustains them through temporary periods of joy."

Today it makes me laugh to look back. I have rediscovered my core brand, but at the time, I felt very confused within myself. Sadness seemed to fill me, even though I would always keep a smile on my face. You can ask folks I was around back then, people whom I worked with, and they will probably describe my brand in a way that was opposite to the brand that was deep inside me and the one I had understood in my youth. I lost the ability to embrace the paradox, and I thought life was adhering to a strict, consistent path for decisions and living.

And trust me, as one does the work in figuring out one's brand and then matches their life to that brand, the process can and probably will be wrenching. For me, it included career change, divorce, an upheaval in how I understood my Catholic faith, a change in relationship with my children—basically, all the important elements in my life.

If you dig deep and reevaluate your brand when you feel off-kilter, this exploration will likely change all aspects of your life. For most of us, it is not just one part of our lives that is disconnected from our brands—it is every part that needs to be readjusted. I often tell people that a starting point in understanding their brands is to see what the gulf is between their journals and their actual lives. For organizations, that gulf is the canyon that might exist between the mission they started with and how their businesses are being run today. The wider the gulf between what you write in your journal (or in dusty mission statements) and the daily steps you take in your life, the less successful you will be and the less you will have joy in your life.

It is not only that we might be pursuing the wrong career, or be trapped in the wrong relationship, or have the wrong circle of friends. In some way, our trouble probably lies in all of those things. As I began to figure all that out, I knew intuitively that changes needed to be made. Sometimes those changes just came naturally and without much thought. But sometimes the changes involved deep introspection and were painstaking.

You shouldn't think that a brand has to do only with Coke, or Nike, or Apple, or a president, or a political party. The most important brand you will ever connect with or understand is your own. The first step in that brand analysis is in diving deep within yourself and discovering who you are under the surface. Values and brands are key for companies and for campaigns, key for leaders at all levels, and they are key to navigating successfully in a world that seems a bit out of control. And it all starts with understanding that the path to leadership is in embracing the paradox.

Though there are many conflicting values we must learn to balance in order to build a successful brand and achieve the ability to lead, I want to focus on eight areas in which embracing the paradox is key, areas we will explore in each of the ensuing chapters. These eight pillars of paradox will provide anyone the insight in how to lead organizations, businesses, groups, our families, and the country as whole, forward in a new way. It is these eight that will be indicators for who is likely to thrive in the decades ahead in our country.

Understanding the paradoxes will hopefully get us past the divisiveness, gulfs, and bitterness that exist so much in our politics and in our country today. Because we have lost our ability to hold in balance a paradox of values and different ways, we have degenerated into an us-versus-them culture. This is reflected in our vitriolic partisan politics, in race discussions and relations, in a misunderstanding between the sexes, in a generational rift, and in economic instability and inequity. It is almost as though the country is in the midst of a terrible divorce.

And divorce is never easy—whether it involves a country or an individual.

Divorce is an ordeal for anyone involved, even in the most agreeable circumstances. Having been through two divorces, I unfortunately have pretty good experience with the ups and downs of this process. Yes, I am twice divorced, but I never saw myself that way when I first got married. I believed that marriage was for life. Each of my divorces was heart-wrenching, because I was with a wonderful woman. As mentioned, people who have been married more than once are the ultimate optimists.

Each time, I thought I had failed my spouse, my family, my God, and myself. In spite of what so many social commentators say, I have never met anyone who went through this process easily and happily. It is a loss no matter how you slice it, especially the loss of a dream and the hope of a lifelong loving commitment. I have learned that the test of relationships is not in the crisis but in the quiet. Each time, I was married to a wonderful woman. In my marriages, we were always good at the crisis, but many times, it was the quiet moments that were uncomfortable and tested the connection.

But my personal experience has given me some insight into leadership, organizations, and politics. So often in our battles in life, we approach things in a totally dualistic way. We see things as us versus them, me versus you, the right way versus the wrong way. We see everything as a dynamic of winners and losers. We throw out the truth of the paradox. We do this in our personal relationships and in our professional and political lives.

In divorce, it is so easy to fall in the trap of "this is mine" and "if you win, then I must lose." Or if I win, then you feel like you have lost. The attorneys we hire encourage those battle lines being drawn. They make a living off the fight of me versus you. We fight over money, assets, blame, and time with our children. Our laws in most states reflect this dualistic approach to divorce.

If we allow it, this seems to be the way the normal process unfolds. Many times, our friends and families encourage a fight like this. Their intentions are often good, but it comes down to winners and losers. Unless we step back and really figure out what is in the best interest of all involved, especially if there are children, the cycle will continue. This is tough to do, but it is the only course with which we can break the pattern and find a new way. We need to quiet the fight within us and seek a more holistic approach to overcoming the difficulty.

We see this unfold in our economy, where businesses see other businesses as competitors that have to be vanquished. We see it in how many businesses approach their employees; often they see them as cost centers rather than as an essential part of the wholeness of the entire enterprise. When a business looks at the world in a dualistic way, then why wouldn't they cut benefits, or cut jobs, and treat others in a way where everything is about winning and losing?

I was on the board of a Catholic charity health system whose mission was to serve the poor and vulnerable in our community of central Texas, but discussions often devolved into seeing other hospitals in the community as competitors rather than as organizations whom we might partner with to serve a similar, bigger purpose. There was also a constant struggle between living out our mission and being financially responsible—a conundrum that didn't always resolve itself into an easy binary choice. It is such a "human" natural reaction, even when in the best possible circumstances, to see the world in this us-versus-them dichotomy.

And the same reaction seems to be true in our state and national politics.

Why does it seem that both major political parties in this country behave like two parents with children going through a bad and bitter divorce?

In this analogy, each party represents one opposing parent in a bad divorce, where the voters are the children.

Interestingly, it is as if one parent lived in Washington, DC, the other lived in New York City, and the children lived in cities and communities around the country. The parents are fighting over the spoils of the divorce, are name-calling, and are using the children as pawns in the process.

In the current political and economic environment, Washington, DC, and New York City continue to do fine. Each of the two legacy parties protects Wall Street and the big banks and business, on the one hand, and encourages the federal government to grow, on the other hand. The politicians seem to be doing fine, and the lawyers involved seem to be getting richer. All the while, voters in Detroit, St. Louis, San Jose, Milwaukee, Phoenix, or Wimberley, Texas, continue to suffer.

When you look at the worlds of Washington, DC, and New York City the way you might look at two bitter spouses, it's as if the national economic struggles have never happened there. Home values have skyrocketed in those places, salaries are good, and retail and small businesses do not seem to have suffered. The opposite is true for voters outside of these two metropolitan areas, however. Home values either have dropped or have seen no appreciable rise, wages are stagnant, and people can't afford to do much shopping. There is a canyon between the experiences of New York City and DC, on the one hand, and the rest of the country, on the other hand. For the past twenty-five years or so, the vast majority of the country has not seen any economic gain.

Neither party is thinking about the voters first in this process; it is just using the voters to gain advantage over the opposing party, much like bitter divorcing parents. In the end of this kind of process, the children suffer, and the only ones who really benefit in the short term are the two parents. In the long term, no one really wins.

And the media, in many instances, acts like the divorce attorneys representing the opposing parties. They aren't trying to encourage agreement; rather, like many lawyers in divorces, they are encouraging the fight, raising the level of emotion and anger, and hoping the fight lasts as long as possible. The media, like a divorce lawyer, gains financial advantage in a long and bitter battle.

In divorces, there is a better way. There is a collaborative process, where the spouses, even though they disagree, think of the best interests of the children involved first and foremost. There are places for mediation, where a more thoughtful and heartfelt approach is allowed to foster. In this new way, each spouse lays down their sword and isn't interested in winning first but in making sure the kids are impacted as positively as possible through the divorce and its aftermath.

And in this collaborative process, the lawyers involved don't encourage bitterness; rather, they discourage it. They try to come up with innovative solutions that are best for the kids. Discussions are calm, and at each point, the question is constantly asked whether what is getting decided is in the children's best interest.

Leaders in business and politics could learn from this. Businesses can learn from other businesses and organizations that see all the parts, including their competitors in the marketplace, as integral parts of the whole. The two political parties and the media should take a lesson from this collaborative process and employ it in our politics. They should think of the folks in Detroit or Wimberley first.

Even though the parties disagree, the disagreement doesn't need to be bitter and harsh. The media should do more to encourage collaboration, as opposed to encouraging the fight. After all, both parties share the same ends: a healthy economy, a strong national defense, and a sense of national pride. Where the parties differ is on the means to the end. So shouldn't the parties get along more and fight less?

Yes, it feels as if our economy and politics today and what is happening to voters throughout the country is like what happens to kids going through a bad divorce. But as we come to realize the negative effects that this polarized process has on the voters, we will turn to a more cooperative and collaborative process. Having gone through that collaborative process myself personally, I know it is very hard and that it seems much easier to just fight, but in the end, the "kids" are better off when the swords are sheathed.

To find a leadership model that doesn't default into dualistic thinking, pointing fingers, and dividing people requires embracing the paradox. Not in choosing one side or the other but in finding the balance among what seem as opposites. Or in creating something unique, whether party or business, that establishes an entirely new way.

In the chapters ahead I would like to focus on the following eight areas and the importance of our ability to embrace the paradox in each: reconciling fear and love, truth and uncertainty, confidence with humility, heart versus head decisions, big vision and local action, idealism and realism, boundaries combined with openness, and delegation and accountability.

For each of these eight, I would like to delve into how leadership isn't about picking one or the other but requires building a brand that encompasses the conflict. I want to create a model for leadership that doesn't force folks into having to pick one way or the other for now and forever. I want people to be able to embrace the paradox and be open to the best decision in the moment—whether you are a president, a preacher, a profit-oriented businessperson, or just a plain person trying to lead your own life with success and joy and peace.

CHAPTER THREE

FEAR/LOVE

President Franklin Roosevelt famously said in the midst of the Great Depression, "The only thing we have to fear is fear itself." He had this partially correct. The only thing we have to fear is not acknowledging the fear we have. Fear itself isn't the problem. Acting as though fears weren't real or just pushing through fears as if they had no consequences is—and is a major recipe for bad decision making and bad leadership. The most powerful fears in life don't have to be real to be powerful. In fact, most of our fears are actually less real than we know. As Mark Twain once said, "I've lived through some terrible things in my life, some of which actually happened."

I watched with great interest and commented on for the news media the presidential contests over the past ten years. Two of these stand out to me particularly: the open contests in 2008 and 2016. The Democratic presidential primary in 2008 pitted then US Senator Barack Obama against US Senator and former First Lady Hillary Clinton. The unfolding of these two primary campaigns in 2008 was a clear sign of what America faces today and what our leaders are going to be required to do to meet the needs of our citizens. There were many interesting dynamics at play, but I want to focus on the one involving fear and love (or hope).

Hillary Clinton did very well in this 2008 race and ended up losing a very close contest. She did this by speaking passionately to many Democratic voters' fears. She talked of the economic fears they had, the fears of being left behind by our American system, and the fears of what the future held for their families. However, she was never able to clearly transition her message into what voters were hoping for or into what they loved and wanted in their lives in America. She mirrored their fears without showing them her vision for a new promised land as Americans.

Barack Obama did an admirable job in 2008 speaking to voters' hopes and dreams. He won, though he never fully connected with what voters were afraid of. His broad campaign was about hope and the America we love. He spoke to the optimistic side of Democratic voters' nature and laid out a path forward for the country. Where he didn't connect well with most Americans was in his inability to reflect back to them what their fears were, to assure them that he understood at a gut level what their anxieties and concerns were all about. Without affirming and empathizing with those fears, Obama never gave Americans a solid sense that he knew what the pitfalls were. He won, though he never fully connected with what voters were afraid of.

In the 2016 presidential race, Donald Trump came up with the optimistic slogan "Make America Great Again," but much of his language, tone, and appeals were to people's fears. This worked particularly well in the industrial Midwestern states, where economic angst and fear were rampant. In the end, these states gave Trump an Electoral College victory, though he lost the national popular election by nearly three million votes. Clinton, on the other hand, seemed to have overlearned the lessons of 2008 and didn't speak at all to these voters' fears. She tried to make a status quo argument of hope. Voters in these Midwestern states seemed unclear about her message and felt she didn't understand what they were going through in their lives. She had no connection on fear this time around, and her message of hope lacked a genuine feel, unlike what President Obama had been able to convey.

Fear is a powerful vehicle that we can and must touch on in life. Our fears are almost ancestral. When we touch on our fears, they resonate so powerfully. We all have them. In order to form connections with or have compassion for someone, you have to understand their fears. And you certainly can't comfort someone without understanding their fears.

As they communicate with the public or within their organizations, leaders can focus on fears and achieve some success. But this type of success is really only about dividing the country and pitting one group against another group. We have seen this dynamic play out in discussions by Republicans and Democrats in pointing fingers and casting blame.

A fear-based message was dramatically clear in the 2016 presidential election, and it is clear in the current Trump administration. This has also unfolded in race conversations and law enforcement, where each side uses fear to try to force accountability on the other. Some media outlets use fear as a motivator to achieve ratings or to rile up folks in anger. We have also seen fear used in faith conversations pitting Christians against Muslims—with disastrous and far-reaching consequences.

And that is the problem with using only fear to connect with others. By converting those fears directly to anger and then to action, you achieve temporary victories without giving people an optimistic path of hope to something they love. Fear alone always settles into hate. And hate takes us only backward.

Hope alone can achieve some success for a leader. As naturally optimistic Americans who have a can-do spirit, we naturally gravitate toward hope. Hope is what our country was founded on and built with through very hard times. Our hopefulness is why we have achieved great heights—putting a man on the moon, promoting techno-logical innovations that have improved the lot of citizens around the world, or providing a standard of living unheard of in the history of the world. But hope and love alone get drowned out and forgotten when others are preaching fear and hate and division. Without connecting on some level with people's fears, hope can sit too meekly amid the daily communications coming at Americans.

Obama was about hope when Hillary was about fear in 2008, and neither found the voice that could intertwine both at the time. Trump had a hope slogan but fear mes-saging in 2016. He could not convince a majority of voters that he was coming from a place of love. Fear can divide and win in the short term, and hope can unite and succeed temporarily, but it is in bridging these two and wrapping them together as a paradox that real leadership affects authentic change in the world and in our lives. Looking ahead, identifying these leaders who wrap an understand-ing of hope and love with a realistic understanding of the challenges facing us is incredibly important.

This paradox of integrating fear and love as leaders requires the ability to do this in the small circles of our lives as well as in the larger circles of our communities and country. It's strangely easier to speak to a crowd of one thousand rather than just one. But you have to be able to form those personal, intimate relationships. Leadership and embracing the paradox of integrating love and fear is about building from the most intimate circles and then moving outward. That is how we learn to do it. That is where leadership begins and where it can be manifested forward.

It has taken me many years and many heartbreaking moments to figure out the intertwining of love and fear, trying to hold the balance of that paradox. I recall vividly my first time of walking the path of fear and love simultaneously.

One sunny Saturday afternoon long ago in Michigan was that moment for me.

I think I was thirteen, though those years have a tendency to blend into one another. Looking back, I find it hard to tell the difference between twelve and fourteen. But certainly, at the time, that difference was exceptionally meaningful. Whatever age I was exactly, I was not yet a man. At least I didn't see myself that way.

As children, we tend to run from fear or to just do what some authority demands. We've almost all been trained to be obedient to authority. As children—and as adults—we many times avoid standing up to our fears and to authority. We talk ourselves into a go-along-to-get-along behavior. At some point, all of us go through a rite of passage that enables us to become stronger in ourselves regardless of the consequences. We embrace our own manhood or womanhood in the true meaning and depth of what that is.

My father had just finished working in the yard. He worked long days in his "paid" job, which for nearly his entire adult life was in the auto industry in Detroit, and then he worked more at home on the weekends. Having eleven children, he had a lot to do in and around the house. We kids had been given chores, and Pop (that's what we called him) would make sure we would get them done, sometimes by force. But he would always do more than manage or yell. He would also help move large rocks or do what was physically necessary to complete the job. But on this day he was tired and was taking a break.

He was on the patio in the back of the house, relaxing as he always did after yard work. He was sitting in a faded-green, rickety lawn chair, wearing a cap to shield his eyes, reading the *Detroit News*, drinking a cup of coffee (probably the ninth that day!), and smoking a cigar. (Unfortunately, one of the habits I have picked up over the years is a fondness for the ritual enjoyment of cigars. Something else I can blame on my pop, just to avoid my own responsibility.)

I watched my pop thoughtfully from an open window two stories above him. Two stories, because it was one of those homes with an exposed basement, so it was a long way from the upstairs bedrooms to the patio below. I had observed from this vantage point many, many times before. But for some reason, this day was different.

Two of my brothers were in the room with me, and we were joking around, as was our custom. We were talking big about how much of a tyrant Pop was and how we were going to tell him off. He gave us quite a few physical and emotional beatings with a belt, a stick, or his mouth along the way, and we often feared him. We loved him but were afraid of him. We were sure brave when he was preoccupied, but something about this moment was hitting me differently that day. I turned to my two brothers at the window and said I would be right back. I ran downstairs to the pantry by the kitchen and grabbed a thick plastic garbage bag and raced back upstairs. I went into the bathroom as my brothers watched and said, "I have an idea."

Not really thinking it through at the moment, I filled up the garbage bag with as much water as it could hold and I could carry. I waddled over to the window of the upstairs bedroom, water dripping on our bedroom floor, and with all the energy I could muster, I swung the bag up and over the windowsill. Then I held onto the bag while it hung out of the open window.

Pop was directly below, enjoying a serene, relaxing moment of his own. The smoke from his cigar mixed with the steam from his hot coffee, floating up into the sky as he calmly perused the paper. I held the bag over him, a good twenty feet above, and paused while my brothers stared at me. From their eyes, I could tell they thought I was crazy or was just kidding—and maybe I was.

I debated a long time in my own mind what to do. And then something clicked, and I said to myself, "If I am going to be a man, get through some fear, and find love and respect for myself, I need to let it go." And with that thought, my hands unclasped, and the twenty-five-plus pounds of water in the garbage bag was gone from the upstairs window, falling majestically below.

As I recall, I looked down both with satisfaction, knowing that I had crossed the line from fear to courage, and with disbelief. "Oh shoot, I can't believe I just did that!" The "water bomb" descended slowly. I had a thousand thoughts going through my head and a bag of mixed feelings in my body.

The heavy garbage bag of water hit my father point blank on the head, knocking his hat off, dislodging him from the chair, soaking his paper, sending his coffee cup flying, and breaking his lit cigar. And there I was with two of my brothers looking out the window at this great "success" as Pop looked up at me in shock, then disbelief, and then anger.

In seconds, I fully realized what I had done and the consequences I was about to face. My pop shot up, ran into the house, and chased me down. I got the belt on the backside that I expected. Between whackings, Pop kept asking me why I did it. I didn't have a ready answer. I didn't have the words I needed about fear and love—just the feeling.

That night as I lay down in my bunk bed, sore from the belt whips, and shifted uncomfortably between my sheets, one of my brothers across the room in his bed looked at me and said, "I can't believe you did that." I smiled to myself. My brother asked me if it was worth it, and I replied without hesitation, "Yes."

I knew things would be different between my pop and me after that and, in some ways, between my brothers and me. But most importantly, the way I felt about myself was different. I knew then that I had the courage within me to do something that I could expect punishment for and get through it. I knew that I could take on authority (even in a ridiculous and rather unreasonable form) and live to see another day.

Was I an adult at that point? Was I now a man? No. I knew, though, that I was leaving behind this stage of my life of unquestioning acceptance and was beginning to move on to another. And once you do that, once you journey from one station toward another on the train track of life, you really can't ever go back. It can't be the same. You are now drawn inevitably to the next stop, because you realize you have stepped off the platform you always knew.

Courage through fear comes in small steps. Even our sophomoric attempts (like the Garbage Bag incident, as it became known in our family) are important moments of definition in one's life. Something stirs within us, and we are given a choice between facing the fear of dropping the bag, or not. I knew then that rationally I should not have done it. But something in me—in my heart, I guess—said that if I walked away from that moment, I would have passed a chance to be taller in my being.

I still wonder about that thirteen-year-old and what he was thinking.

Today we each struggle with what it means to be a leader. Deep down we wonder about what it means to be a man or woman in today's society. We send confusing signals to one another about what we want, but in the end a big step toward discovering what we really want and who we are is facing our own fears out of a place of love. It is looking at our own vulnerabilities and crossing the line when we are given the right moment with courage. Being and accepting our vulnerable nature is a sure sign of an authentic leader who can bridge fear and love.

We have to develop the ability to approach our own fears and our loves with a sense of connection. We cannot talk ourselves out of our fears, nor can we power through them. We have to spend time reflecting on ourselves, to see our fears clearly, to hold them, and then to make decisions out of a sense of love. First for ourselves, and then for others. And then we can lead going forward.

It is in our self-examination that we can discover the hopes and fears that exist in our communities and country writ large. Leaders in business, politics, charity, or church need to see and understand the fears of others, give voice to those fears so we each feel understood, and develop a forward-looking message based in hope and love. Embracing a new way of leadership in the twenty-first century, our leaders will need to understand the paradox of fear and love in themselves to connect with the deep levels of fear and love within each of us.

Leadership for our country that unites us will need to embrace this paradox of feeling both fear and love together. Campaigns and candidacies purely based in fear will continue to divide us and create increasing levels of discord and disconnection. Messages based solely on love will wilt in the field of fear messaging. Leadership requires being comfortable in the paradox of love and fear.

CHAPTER FOUR

TRUTH/ UNCERTAINTY

Oftentimes when I give talks to public relations people, press secretaries, or anyone who interacts with the media or with the public, I tell the audience that there are four or five cardinal rules in communicating with news representatives or with the public at large. I say the first rule is "Tell the truth, be honest."

I am always amazed that half the audience writes that rule down. As though that were original, innovative advice rather than a fundamental tenet of the job.

Gandhi once said that happiness is when what we think, what we say, and what we do are in alignment. I would add that, in addition to happiness, integrity and the pursuit of truth is what this alignment is fundamentally all about. Today we have few leaders interested in integrity as a driving force, whether in our politics, businesses, or in most of public life. It seems we have settled for dodging the truth, creating spin, or having a biased take on what is going on in the world.

We have lost the value we were raised on of speaking the truth—especially to powerful forces. And without a grasp of the truth, we have no way of making informed decisions on what is best for ourselves or for our communities. We certainly can't live an authentic life or be an authentic leader without a firm commitment to integrity and the truth. Authenticity is probably the single most important value that citizens desire in leaders, especially at this time in American history. Unfortunately, people have shown that they will move toward false mirages of bravado and simplicity, because they think that represents authenticity.

Each of us has biases that we carry with us in life. We must try to overcome them if we want to be at all objective in our worldview. These biases come from where we were born, the schools we attended, our religions, our sex, our race, and much of our upbringing. I would argue that a lifelong pursuit for every one of us is to try to see the truth, even as we passionately advocate for causes we deeply believe in. It is very difficult in today's communication environment to sort through the ways our biases affect us while we uphold our convictions.

Sociologists use the term *confirmation bias* to describe

the natural human tendency to seek information that confirms our existing biases and ignore information that makes us uncomfortable because they run counter to our preexisting opinions or prejudices. With cable television, satellite radio, the Internet, and social media, it has become much easier to seek confirming information. We have greater access to information and knowledge today, but it seems we are further away from the truth. We are a more knowledgeable society but a less wise one. We have greater ability to gather data points but less ability, or availability of wisdom, to figure out what is true, and then to put that truth into a context to live by with integrity.

Finding the truth in a very uncertain world at an incredibly confusing time is a difficult task that doesn't end. Inevitably, the debate surrounding the truth seems to be between two opposing camps: absolutists versus relativists. Absolutists insist that there is a truth that is clear, definable, and always consistent. Their worldview is incredibly black and white. Absolutists have "discovered" the truth—which for them always was, and always is, the truth—and there is no room for debate.

For relativists, on the other hand, there really is no set truth. Everyone's truth is different. You have a truth. Another person may have a different truth. It is all relative. There are no universal truths or any defined reality that we can count on other than whatever each individual believes.

I believe that truth is a paradox, not completely absolute

or completely relative, but a bit of both. There are discoverable truths in life, but truth is a long and arduous journey. Truth isn't a stopping point, where we just rest and relax into what we have discovered. Yes, we can find the truth, and yes, there are elements of the world that are true for all of us. But we must accept that much in these truths isn't black and white. And uncertainty is a huge part of the path we must walk.

We must seek to discover what the truth is, but we must not comfortably close our minds, believing that we have it all. Discovering the truth is like going through a fog and finding our way, while still understanding that there may be more to learn. That there may be more exploring to do. And that in the moment we think we have our hands firmly on the truth, something can change or adjust so that we may need to alter our viewpoint. We discover truth as we see uncertainty.

For leaders, the question becomes: Do you want to discover the truth, or do you just want to find some evidence that supports your preexisting biases as you enact your worldview? The truth in politics, culture, and business is too often not seen as an end in itself but as a tactic one can wield to accomplish some agenda. Leaders need to be open to the process of discovering the truth, so that they can make the most informed decisions based on that truth. If new information becomes available, they must be strong enough and open enough to change the decision they have already made.

People often ask me how I found the courage to publicly break with the president of the United States in April 2007 on the front page of the *New York Times*. How was I ready for that moment, and what was going through my mind? And did I feel disloyal, having worked for President Bush and then, in many people's minds, betraying him? Well, that is all a bit of a story.

The road to that moment of truth in the *New York Times* had many stops along the way, each of which led to the next moment. Life is funny; small windows of seeing and living the truth open up, and either we seize that opportunity, even in a small way, or we let it pass. And one window leads to another window and another, and pretty soon you are in a much different spot from where you were when you started. You have moved closer to the truth through the fog.

I didn't get up one day, after years of working for President Bush (I was involved in his first campaign for president in 2000, worked the years in between, and was chief strategist in 2004), and decide that I was going to call up the *New York Times* and get a few things off my chest. If someone had suggested that plan, I would have laughed. My questioning of his leadership was a gradual process, and I had to gather my voice in small ways along the way, letting God or the universe guide what needed to happen next, before I could speak what I thought was true.

My questions began during Bush's first term, when I

wondered if we really needed a second round of tax cuts. I felt that policy was going to fiscally hurt the country in the end and wasn't fair to all. I pondered after 9/11 why we weren't asking the country for a common sacrifice. I wondered why we weren't laying out a vision of really changing Washington then, when the country was universally supportive of reform. I had actually inquired in a number of calls and meetings at the White House why we weren't asking the country for more active involvement, like what had happened during World War II with war bonds or scrap metal collections. I was told to get back into my lane.

In 2004, while I was intimately involved in President Bush's reelection, I began to have grave misgivings about where we were headed. The Abu Ghraib scandal was a telling moment for me. I had thought we were the accountability administration, but we weren't really holding leaders accountable. I thought Secretary of Defense Don Rumsfeld should have been fired at that point or been asked to resign. I communicated my belief to key folks at the White House and got no real answer. During the reelection campaign, I questioned why we were getting involved in the gay marriage issue at such a high level, and I tried to tell the people at the White House that it wasn't where the country wanted to go.

But I was a team player, so I buckled down and rationalized that once Bush was reelected, we could do all the things we had promised. Most importantly, we could bring the country together and get past the partisanship, my real goal. As I said to the *New York Times* in 2007, working at such a high level and in that atmosphere is a lot like a relationship. You fall for someone and want to believe in all the best parts of them, in what the relationship could be. You see red flags, but you forgive too quickly or you rationalize too easily. Oh, she mistreated the dog—well, work must be bad. Or, why is he yelling at the kids? Oh, he must be sad about something… It soon spirals until you find yourself in a place you never expected to be.

Eventually we awake to reality, find a level of needed personal accountability, take a hard look at ourselves and the relationship, and say, "This isn't what I wanted or what I thought it was." And at that point, we have to figure out what we do. I hit this juncture after I got back home to Austin and had time to reflect after the reelection. The day after Election Day in 2004, I put a handwritten note on the door of my office at the campaign, which just said "GTT." That means "Gone to Texas" and is what many pioneers posted on their doors in other states as they set out to Texas to start a new life.

And, as I settled back in Texas, I began to figure out my voice and where my heart was. I began to discover the truth, and my own truth.

In 2006, I was asked about the gay marriage issue, and I said publicly for the first time that I thought the way it was being used was wrong and was a mistake. At the end of that year, I told the Republican National Committee that I no longer wanted to do work for them. After the California governor's race, in a conference room at the University of California in early 2007, I took this all a step further.

I had served as chief strategist for Governor Arnold Schwarzenegger in his reelection campaign. We were having a post-election forum in Berkeley to discuss the campaign. A young kid in a T-shirt and frayed jeans stood up at this gathering and basically asked how I could sleep at night, given all the young people who had died in Iraq, knowing that I had helped elect and reelect Bush and Cheney. He said something about blood for oil and tyrants and how Bush had destroyed our country. The moderator wanted to ignore his question and move on quickly, but I said I wanted to respond. I started by saying that he might not know I had a son in the army who was about to be deployed to Iraq. This fact is what kept me up at night.

I then went on to say in a very general way, without really mentioning President Bush, that sometimes in life we have hopes and dreams and expectations and they don't turn out the way we want. When that happens, we have to figure out what to do. I was troubled by how the presidency had turned out. I didn't say much more.

The *Los Angeles Times* did a little blog post on that speech, basically saying that it looked like I was beginning to question the administration. My friend Evan Smith, who at the time was running *Texas Monthly* (a great magazine, incidentally), noticed this blog post and called me up to write a piece for their magazine on Bush's legacy. He said a bunch of folks were contributing, and it would be a good forum. I would be just one of many critical voices. I said, "Sure."

Well, it turned out my short piece (which again was a soft criticism) drew the most attention, because I was the only Bush insider to raise real concerns. The *Washington Post* picked the story up, but then I didn't hear a word for a few weeks. Finally, a friend and respected journalist at the *New York Times* called me, saying they thought it would be an interesting story of how I went from insider and loyalist to critic. I agreed.

He flew down to Austin, and we had a three-hour lunch at a Tex-Mex restaurant not far from the state capitol. Funny thing about the location of that restaurant is that it was a block from where the Bush campaign in 2000 had been located. I said to the *Times* reporter that it was amazing that I'd come so far but had made it only three hundred feet from that effort.

At that lunch, I talked freely and openly about how I thought the war was a mistake. About how we were supposed to have united the country, yet the country was now even more polarized. The reporter took notes and then flew back to New York. He finished the story and then called me on Saturday morning, saying that it was about to hit the web. I might want to turn off my phone speaker. I said, "Okay, but why?"

He said this was a big story and that it was going to be on the front page of the Sunday *Times*.

"Really, I didn't think this was that big of a deal," I said. In my mind, I hadn't done anything courageous or controversial. I'd just spoken the truth as I saw it after going on a very long journey of discovery.

Whether or not I thought the story mattered, the reporter said it was a big story and it was going to be above the fold. In journalistic terms, a story being on the front page and above the fold is about as high profile as it can be.

I made a decision at that point to do little to no additional media. I thought I had said my piece and that it could stand on its own. I didn't want to make this about me. Though I disagreed with President Bush in a variety of ways, I thought he was a decent man with a good heart. I also knew he had given me an opportunity in politics that I would always be grateful for. I didn't want anyone to think I was profiting off my break or trying to become a media star.

I lost quite a bit of income because of this break with the president. Some business folks didn't want to be associated with me anymore. I did get tons of interview requests but ignored nearly every single one, although a few weeks later, I decided to do a short NPR interview. As my thinking was evolving, that was a good, thoughtful

Dolly's Bookstore

510 Main Street
P.O. Box 28018
Park City, UT 84060
(435) 649-8062
dollysbookstore.com

Thanks for shopping with us!

Cust: **None**

| 08-May-17 4:28p | Clerk: liza |
| Trans. #: 10398892 | Reg: 2 |

| 9781544500324 | *New Way: Embracing T* |
| 1 @ $14.95 | $14.95 |

| Sub-total: | $14.95 |
| Tax @ 8.450%: | $1.26 |

| **Total:** | **$16.21** |

* Non-Tax Items
Items: 1   *Units: 1*

Payment Via:

VISA/MC/Discover $16.21

Dolly's Bookstore Return Policy:
EXCHANGE or STORE CREDIT ONLY
Within 30 days of purchase
Merchandise must be in excellent condition!

(and less sensational) forum to discuss my insights. I was even approached by a New York publishing firm to write a quick book on how Bush had broken my heart, which I promptly turned down.

Many Bush folks reacted very negatively to my speaking my truth, and they ended their friendships with me. Some stayed my friends but wondered why I had gone public. My rationale is a little bit like karma. Since I had been a public advocate for Bush, I didn't feel I could quietly go away and not say something. I thought the scales of the universe demanded something more than silence, so I needed to do something public. Everyone has to answer that question in their own way, and I don't judge how anyone else determines their own path.

Some of the Bush folks questioned my loyalty. I have often wondered where people think our loyalties should really lie. Are we supposed to be loyal to an institution or to a party or to a person? Or are we called to a deeper loyalty to our own integrity, a loyalty to the truth as we see it? And when being loyal to a person or a party conflicts with our truth, don't we have to try to understand our own journey with integrity?

The road to truth isn't normally like Saint Paul's ride to Damascus, where he was struck by a bolt of light from the sky in one huge moment. It is usually a series of steps or windows, a path through the fog that present themselves. We have to figure out if we are ready to take steps in those moments. In those smaller steps, we are actually led to the bigger truth.

In life, we have to pay attention not just to the big splashes but to those subtle messages and windows to the truth that open up. The truth is usually a staircase with many steps. It is okay to pause, absorbing the uncertainty, if we are tired along the way. Pausing enables us to gather ourselves and our strength to keep moving forward. Then as leaders we are ready to make decisions based on the truth so that we can improve our world, or the world at large, in an informed way.

CHAPTER FIVE

CONFIDENCE/ HUMILITY

In today's world, it seems that the idea of a strong but humble servant leader thriving and succeeding is improbable, possibly impossible, and a dream of a long-forgotten era. Leading in our own lives with a sense of both confidence and humility seems difficult enough, but expecting leaders in public to pattern that paradox for our country seems a bridge too far.

We watched in the last presidential election a candidate succeed with bravado, braggadocio, and immense ego. We wonder if that is the pattern leaders must follow in order to thrive today. I believe the pendulum has swung so far in one direction, however, that in order to be a successful leader in the twenty-first century, as it swings back, you must be a leader who can sit in the intersection of confidence and humility.

It is true that leaders need to have a healthy sense of self. A bit of an ego is probably inevitable. But we need to distinguish between an ego that enables us to walk tall in the world and arrogance. Arrogance makes others feel smaller. Arrogance is when we hold power over others in order to weaken them. Arrogance is not connection. Rather, what our country hungers for is humility *with* confidence, which will create the connection between leaders and their constituents.

In this momentous, turbulent time, servant leadership is also important on a personal level. There are many smaller paradoxes that are going to have to be embraced in order for each of us to be one of the servant leaders the country needs. We need to be able to go both inward and outward on a daily basis. From moment to moment, we have to practice acts of surrender while being proactive. Most importantly, we must go out into the world from a place of abundance, even while we feel within ourselves a place of lack or scarcity.

A few years ago, scientists discovered that not only is our universe continuing to expand outward, but the expansion is also accelerating. As the universe expands at increasing speeds, the expansions in our own life gather steam at an accelerated pace. In response, for many of us, either we get caught up in the noise and activity of the outside world, or we turn inward and say it is all too much to face, with too many stresses. We seek calm and peace, isolated solely within ourselves. If they desire to change the world at large as well as their own world, however, leaders are going to need to go both outward and inward. Leading will be about achieving positive change in the external world while also being equipped to build an interior life.

If one searches the history of human civilization to discover lessons on the tension of going inward and outward, you don't have to search any further than such people as Jesus or Buddha or Teresa of Ávila or Mahatma Gandhi or Martin Luther King Jr. or Nelson Mandela or Dorothy Day. Each of these leaders had a profound effect on the world, and they also understood that going inward and going outward were equally important. They preached, taught, and led externally, but each of them knew that taking the time to reconstitute inwardly was crucial. They understood that the outward path couldn't be accomplished with any integrity without an inward journey. One can't confront all of the external demands and conflicts without an inner sanctuary.

In close proximity to the inward/outward dynamic is the idea that a leader must be able to be proactive and be prepared to surrender at a moment's notice to "what is." The balance lies in struggling for what is right, just, and good while also practicing acceptance. Though these pursuits seem diametrically opposed to each other, successful authentic, proactive leadership today absolutely requires surrender along with strength.

Many leaders believe that surrender is an act of weakness, of merely giving up, while in reality it is one of the most powerful signs of strength. I have been through many addiction rehab programs with family members. One of the first things you learn in rehab is that the greatest step toward personal power and serenity is learning to practice surrender.

But remember that surrendering does not equal inaction. Some people believe that our communities are in turmoil, America is a mess, and the world is an awful place. They see themselves as tiny cogs in a large system upon which they can have no effect. They believe the only way to maintain their peace is to stay in surrender and not be proactive—even if they tried, they think, it wouldn't have any effect. This perspective is misguided and keeps us from being the leaders the world demands.

We need to ask ourselves from what inner place we are entering the world and how we are being proactive. I have often thought that the way we enter into the world and lead in all the parts of our lives comes either from a place of abundance and surplus within ourselves or from a place of lack or scarcity. Do we share generously what we have, or do we grasp for things to fill the holes within us? Do we enter relationships from a place of self-satisfaction and being enough already, or do we come to a relationship trying to make ourselves whole because we don't feel adequate? Do we give from the surplus we have so we don't feel the need to win, or do we relate to others out of the fear of losing so that we need to seek victories along the roads of our lives? It is from the place of abundance that we can truly be at peace, be humble, and lead.

In his second inaugural address on the verge of winning the Civil War, Abraham Lincoln began to lay out his compassionate vision of how the South should be treated with the words "With malice toward none, with charity for all." Nelson Mandela emerged from spending nearly his entire adult life in prison with the end of apartheid at hand, and even though he had begun a meteoric rise as a popular leader in South Africa, his main message was of reconciliation rather than revenge. These to me are the actions and words of humility in true leaders.

The demonstration of humility is best practiced when a leader is at a high point—when he has great abundance—rather than when he is at a low point or in a position of scarcity. Let me explain.

In the aftermath of losing the 2010 midterm elections, President Obama expressed that mistakes had been made. He was taking responsibility, because he knew his administration had messed up in how they had gone about unfolding the Affordable Care Act. While I could argue that the timing of his acknowledgment could have been much sooner and more forceful, it is good to see a president admit errors.

But this kind of humility when you are down, when you are searching for a way to get back on top, to regain your popularity, does not carry nearly the weight as if he had been more magnanimous and humble when he'd been on top.

The greatest power of humility in bringing positive change to our world exists when a leader engages opponents when he is strong, gives power away when he has plenty, and lifts up the competitors with a strong and compassionate hand. The true measure of humility is how it is exercised when a leader has won, when he is strong and on top, not when he has lost, when he is weak and down.

President Obama (and President Bush in the aftermath of 9/11) each had an opportunity to practice this type of humility while they were in an abundance of power, and both at times chose a more divisive path, where friends were rewarded and political enemies punished.

Because both these presidents didn't have the strength of this brand of humility to actually be "bigger" by sharing political capital when they were "big" in the polls, they became smaller over time and were left with diminished stature and a dysfunctional system in Washington even more polarized than when they arrived. A leadership model based in humility would have practiced a means of governing through some form of national unity on big values and issues. This would have moved the country and our politics forward and given each of them a lasting legacy we could all be proud of.

When President Obama was at his high point in the aftermath of his historic election in 2008 after having resoundingly defeated the Republicans, instead of bringing the opposition in and sharing power, he said, "I won" in response to entreaties on compromise. And with each step forward from then on, the administration sought victories over a weakened and floundering political enemy.

Now we have a new president. His style seems the exact opposite of humility, of going out into the world from a place of abundance. President Trump appears to react out of an insecure place, seemingly wanting to punish opponents and reward friends. So far, at nearly every step where he could have led, interacted broadly, and brought together those who either opposed him or were worried about his leadership, he chose ego instead. This isn't the path of humility, and it definitely isn't the way of uniting us in the common good.

Bridging the paradox of humility and confidence is crucial—and is also exceedingly difficult. Having the capacity to go inward and outward, to surrender and be proactive, and to act from a place of abundance instead of lack is definitely the road less traveled, as Robert Frost might say. In order to accomplish this as a leader, you must have a daily spiritual routine or practice.

For most of my life, I have tried to stay in good physical shape. I did this by being involved in sports when I was younger. When I got older, I had to maintain a high energy level because of my intense work schedule, and because I wanted to stay fit to play with my kids (this was a huge priority for me—and let me tell you that keeping up with kids is much easier when you're in your twenties than when you're in your fifties).

Keeping oneself physically fit includes eating well and implementing a regular exercise regimen. What we put in our body is so important to how we feel. Throughout the year, I try to abstain from things in my diet that I know are probably not good for me. I also want to demonstrate that I am in charge of what I eat or drink. You have to decide who has the power, your food and drinks or your thoughts. I sometimes keep up this regimen for a month or a whole year.

Running was always my thing, and I usually liked to do it in the a.m. I would have a cup of tea, drink some water, get laced up, and go early. I didn't always want to run, but I knew I had to keep it up on a regular basis; otherwise, I would not be where I wanted to be, physically or spiritually. Running always gave me a sense of peace and freedom. There is something about running in the outdoors that touches me deep down.

Here's a trick or a practice I taught myself on exercising over time to keep me going on a consistent basis. On the days I didn't feel like running or going to the gym, I would just tell myself, "Put your gym clothes on, but you don't have to go if you don't want to." Then I would say, "Put your running shoes on, but you don't have to go." Then, "Just drive to the trail or gym, but you can divert for breakfast if you want." Then I would get to the gym and say, "Just go in, and you can sit and read the paper if you want."

By the time I got in, I would basically say, "Well you're here, so go ahead and work out." I know it's a mental trick, but it got me to the trail or gym on the days I didn't feel like working out. Sometimes the best thing we can do is just plan one step ahead when we don't want to do what we know is good for us. Just take that first step of getting dressed and commit no further—then the next step, then the next. So often we get overwhelmed by the energy and effort it will take to get to the end result that we don't take the first step.

I give one piece of advice to friends or family who are struggling to get out of bed or who are so down they don't even have the energy to go through the day. I tell them: Feet, Floor, Coffee, Door. Though I don't drink coffee (weirdly, never in my life have I had a cup), I have been in the same place as those struggling folks. Don't worry about your whole day and what you don't have the energy for. Just get your feet on the floor, grab some coffee, and get out the door. That will move you in a huge way toward embracing the day.

So many of us concentrate on keeping our physical muscles in shape with a regular routine of exercise and body building, but we neglect to do the same with our souls and our spiritual sides. If we believe our souls are crucial to who we are, then we should exercise them and take time with them, just as we would our physical bodies. We should put together a regimen for our souls if we really want to keep those "muscles" in shape and prepared for life. What are our feet, floor, coffee, and doorsteps for our spiritual sides?

Most of the major spiritual paths in the world encourage or demand a regular routine of prayer or meditation. This is something I learned every day on my pilgrimage. The morning or evening prayers of Christianity or Judaism, the meditation of Hinduism or Buddhism, or the regular call to prayer of Islam—each have an instruction of staying in regular connection to the universe or to God. Even if you aren't religious, exercising your spiritual side is essential for a fulfilled life. It gives you the wherewithal when your physical body is run-down or your emotions feel too overwhelmed to keep going. More importantly, it helps you stay in a place of humility as a leader.

We each must try to keep our soul in shape, like with physical exercise, with a commitment to a regularized form of prayer or meditation. Each of us struggles to find the right time to do that in our busy schedule. Having gone through various ways and paths and trying different routes, I realized a few years back when is the perfect time of day for me to do this.

Again, this was my own discovery ten or so years ago. I

figured out that I had to pray or meditate or do some form of contemplation right when I got up and had my tea. If I waited until I had my shower, then I was already in my head, thinking about the day to come. So often the shower we take in the morning hour is the beginning of moving into the full day ahead; it's when we start thinking about all the things we need to do: kid stuff, meetings, errands, etc. We begin making choices about what is ahead in the day. However, it is crucial to catch yourself before the day catches you.

The time between waking and the shower is the perfect moment to say a prayer or sit quietly and meditate. We need to give ourselves twenty or thirty minutes before the shower to just be with ourselves and whatever God we visualize. Or just sit with our connection to the universe.

This time can be as simple as reading a prayer or poem you like, or taking in a reading from a daily meditation book. It can also even be just thinking about a single word. What does *hope* mean to you? What about *love*? *Gratitude*? *Family*? *Connection*? *Community*? *Humility*? It can even be negative words and the feelings they bring up in you; just breathe through them. Just one word can be all you need to meditate on.

You can start with two minutes, and then do five minutes, and then work up to thirty minutes. Just as with physical exercise, you will be amazed after three months at the progress you will have made and how much more centered and better you feel about life. It will make you feel filled with joy and actually more optimistic and powerful. Your soul is in search of a daily connection to yourself, and when they connect, you have a feeling of the divine or the infinite.

As you plan your run or your gym visit, devote some of the time before your shower—as your feet hit the floor, while you grab your coffee, but before the door—to run some laps with your own heart and soul. Soon you will be doing that marathon of spirituality you always dreamed of or wondered about when you read the stories of leaders from the past. Your spiritual growth will help you hold the place of paradox between humility and confidence. Small steps such as this will help you bring about that change you want to see in your own world and in the world at large.

CHAPTER SIX

HEART/HEAD

Leadership demands the ability to tap into the pushes and pulls of two separate and crucial areas of our beings—our hearts and our heads. Making important decisions as a president, head of a business, or family member is dependent on what is going on in our hearts and in our heads. We cannot just push away the whispers of our hearts so we can be logical with our heads. But we also cannot solely go with a gut instinct or blindly follow the passion of our hearts. We must be able to operate in the balance of the two competing places and hold onto that paradox between the two.

Often in life I have been faced with momentous decisions, personal and professional. Too many times, I could not hold the balance of heart and head. I would decide too strongly from one or the other place. Most of the time, it didn't turn out well. In my two divorces, I think I went too quickly with a gut, or heart, decision and didn't give my spouses or myself enough head time to help process through and present in a calm manner. I learned later on that whenever we skip either the head element or the heart element, it catches up to us later on in life. Eventually we have to process what we put off. Whenever I could maintain the balance of the paradox of heart and head, the decision always seemed to work out best. But it wasn't easy.

Sitting by a crackling fireplace in a warm, cozy room on New Year's Eve, overlooking the frozen shore of Lake Superior at the Big Bay Point Lighthouse, I realized that I had to quit my job and sell my share in the company I had founded ten years earlier. Feeling as though I were in the movie *Ice Station Zebra* because of the bitter cold and wicked wind of Michigan's Upper Peninsula, I understood that I had to leave the security of a well-paying business and move to an unchartered and risky place.

When you make decisions from both a heart and a head place, many times the choice comes down to one of security versus opportunity. Or, to put it another way, a choice between one option, which involves little risk and lacks creativity, and the other option, which has purpose and meaning but involves lots of risk and unknowns. Many folks in life want to lead creatively and chart a unique path yet want some guarantee of security. Others love the security of a certain job or relationship but then envy someone who is living creatively.

This thinking gets you into an unfortunate bind. Every time I have taken the risky choice, I was scared—yet every time when I look back, it was the right decision. In this specific case, I had young children from a previous marriage, was newly married for the second time, and had a large home mortgage. But I knew in the snows at that lighthouse that it was time to make a change in my work. My gut was telling it to me, but I knew that my head had to also be in play.

My wife at the time was scared and concerned about what would happen next. How would we pay bills? (And maybe more importantly, what would I do with my time?!) But, like all good friends, she supported me through her fears. Even though we are now divorced, I will always be grateful for that and much, much more. She knew I was unhappy at work and that it was eating me up inside. She knew it was time for me to make a change.

It is a terrible thing when work becomes a time you dread each morning as you rise. When work becomes something you get through as opposed to something you want to do. I remember vividly in my last years of being with the company I had founded, was president of, and had built up from just two of us to over a hundred employees, that on Sunday afternoons a pit in my stomach would start forming. I was anticipating quite negatively going into my job on Monday morning. Sundays are supposed to be a day of rest and joy, but they had become for me a day of anxiety and stress. I don't think that is what God intended for this day, or any day for that matter.

I was tired of arguing with people about what title they needed, or whether or not they needed a window office, or if they really should have a parking spot in the indoor garage or one in the open lot. I got sick of arguing with others in the company about whether we were spending too much money on frivolous things and how we should treat people in the office. I had started in this business to help solve problems of clients, to try to think of creative solutions, and to enjoy my time and have fun. At this point, I was having little if any of that. All I felt I was dealing with was internal problems of our own company.

So on that Monday morning when I got back, I walked into a meeting with my partners and said I had had enough. I was leaving. Shocked, they asked what I was going to do next. "I have no idea" was my most truthful response. Was I scared? Absolutely. Was I certain in my heart? Assuredly. I thought I might teach for a while. Or wander a bit. But I mainly wanted to breathe and find out what my heart said I should do next.

Does everyone have the possibility of leaving their job today? No, and I don't underestimate how people feel anchored to their work or other things in their lives. I understand we all have responsibilities and commitments that often convince us we have to do things we don't want to do. That every day isn't about doing everything we like but about trying to move a step or steps closer to our call-ing. I have learned that what gets in the way for most of us is not commitment but rather fear and a lack of faith in ourselves.

I feel blessed that I could make the choice and then land on my feet. The peace I thought I sought turned into something completely different. A few months later, I went to work for then-Governor George Bush's campaign for president, which had a convoluted heart-and-head path all its own.

When you make a decision that is simultaneously from a heart and head place, it is not as if you ignore logistics or the things that must get done in life. It is a question of when you apply the logistics in the process. I believe most people worry too much about the logistics of making a decision and not enough about what their hearts say or what feeds their souls or the soul of the community or country. Everyone has to decide within themself what they are capable of doing.

So many people counsel us to go through all the logis-tics of the aftermath of a decision in order to determine what we want to do. The decision then becomes about the logistics rather than about the actual decision you need to make. I think we do the opposite when making the right decision—when trying to find that balance in the paradox of heart and head.

Logistics and what happens in your head is very

important, but I have seen many friends and business colleagues who let the complicated logistics tell them what to do. I have seen friends stay in toxic relationships for years and years because the logistical path ahead frightened them. If you are going to end a relationship, decide if it is time. If your job is sucking the life out of you, make that decision. If you believe the mission is central to your business or leadership, then center yourself or your organization on that first, and then discuss rationales later on. Don't use the logistics of what will happen next influence what you should or should not do. Spend time to first determine what your heart says, and then get in touch with the logistics once that is determined.

So much of what happens through the course of our lives is stuff that we have no control over. We don't get to choose where we are born. We don't get to pick the families we are born into. We really don't get to pick what we look like (I know, I know, there are plastic surgeons), the talents we are born with, or the religion to which we are first exposed. So much of life happens for us or to us. But there are a few things we get to choose.

We get to choose the work we do, and we get to choose the relationships we are in. We get to choose the communities we live in, and we get to pick who we want as leaders in our country. And those few choices that we actually have need to be ones that create big happiness; otherwise, the sum total of our few choices we have and the ones we don't have really amounts to only tiny pockets of happiness.

If your work is only 60/40 positive or if the intimate relationship you have is only 55/45 leaning good, then you are doing your entire life a disservice. As I have said, if you are doing a balance sheet analysis of whether you should stay in your job or stay in a relationship, adding up the pros on one side and the cons on the other, then you already are making a mistake and most likely need to make a change in what you are doing. The choices in those things we each get to decide should be so overwhelming that it doesn't feel confusing at all. If it isn't overwhelming joy, then you already know what you need to do. Begin to plan on doing something else.

Yes, the choices I have made of going with overwhelming joy, choices that started in my heart, caused disruption and anger. My partners were not at all happy with me, and my wife was very worried when I decided to quit my work. But I engaged my head quickly in the decision-making process, so that fear turned to courage with a plan emerging ahead. I was able to stay strong enough for long enough, and then new windows opened up—the first window of which was working for the presidential campaign of then-Governor George W. Bush and future President Bush.

In the course of watching President Bush, I realized that he made many decisions from a gut-level place. He was a man of principle and often would lead with his heart. The American public connected very strongly to this and responded positively. This was especially true in the aftermath of the attacks on 9/11. The country was scared and angry and wanted revenge on the perpetrators—an understandable reaction, especially from a human sentiment point of view. A president needs to be able to reflect these emotions back to the country so they feel they are being understood. But a president also needs to employ his head side of the decision process so that long-term effects can be weighed and the logistics can be contemplated.

The president's decision to go to war with Iraq, as well as that of many leaders on both sides of the aisle who supported it, ended up being a colossal mistake, because it came too much from a heart or gut place; President Bush didn't employ the head enough as leader of our country and our place in the world in the long term. Yes, everyone desired an emotional response to 9/11, and we were angry. But a president needs to pause after absorbing the gut feeling or reaction and make decisions from a much colder, rational place. He did not do this. Our country ended up in a prolonged war, costing us trillions of dollars and the lives of thousands of Americans as well as others. Our status in the world to lead has suffered and has limited our options.

President Obama, on the other hand, seemed to rely overly on his head for leading. Many Americans and foreign leaders have had a hard time connecting with him on a heart level, including leaders of Congress. I got to know US Senator Obama in a few meetings I had with him before he ran for president. He came to Austin in 2006 for the Texas Book Festival when his book, *The Audacity of Hope*, had just come out. He asked me for a meeting at the Driskill Hotel.

After that first meeting and the few more in the months following, I was struck by how thoughtful Senator Obama was. I admired much of what he said and his ideas for what he wanted to do about bringing the country together. He also seemed incredibly intelligent. But I could tell that it was his brain that had got him to where he had arrived, and I had a hard time really reading his heart.

I think over the course of President Obama's tenure that the struggles and difficulty in his presidency have been about way too much head and not enough heart, or more succinctly, about his inability to connect consistently with the public at a heart level. Whether it has been in connecting with the American public or in building alliances with congressional leaders, what was lacking was a heart link. The inability to connect with others at a gut level has exacerbated much of the dysfunction that exists in DC. You can't convince your opponent with facts or reasoned arguments until you connect at a heart level, and this is where President Obama's leadership broke down.

President Bush led with his heart most the time, President Obama led with his head most of the time, and while both came to office with a promise of uniting the country, making government work better, and getting past the dysfunction, they have left us more polarized in the aftermath. There are many reasons for this, and the fault doesn't fall totally on either one of them, but not being able to hold the balance of heart and head as a leader is a major reason.

Our next president and leaders of institutions around the country are going to be required to better embrace the paradox of heart and head in decision making and relationship building. Unfortunately, I worry that President Trump is reacting only from a personal, instinctual gut place and that mistakes will be made. We need leaders who are in touch not only with their guts but also in a visceral way with the heart of the country. They must also be disciplined enough to pause and allow their heads to catch up before making purely emotional decisions. They must connect on the heart level with communities and then present logical steps to achieve their goals. Leadership at all levels in the twenty-first century demands the important aspects of heart and head.

It's funny... Growing up, I have always been a huge fan of lighthouses. I visit them wherever I go. There is something romantic and meaningful about a lighthouse to me. Not only do they warn of danger for ships at sea, but they also welcome those ships into a safe harbor. Lighthouses are beacons of hope, safety, and comfort. They are also connected to a response in people's heads and hearts.

That Big Bay Point Lighthouse helped warn me against

staying any longer in a job I didn't like, against losing my way in life, but it also welcomed me into a brand-new harbor I hadn't known was there. Leadership today and in the years ahead will need to be like lighthouses—welcoming us in, warning us of danger, telling us where to go, and doing it from a head-and-heart balanced approach.

CHAPTER SEVEN

BIG VISION/ LOCAL ACTION

I was driving my truck out to west Texas one Christmas Day to spend a little time alone in the Davis Mountains. Listening to country music and enjoying the beautiful scenery, I started thinking about our country and the paradox of values that come with being an American. One set of these paradoxical values is our deep-down sense of rugged individualism *and* our belief in community—that we each are part of a bigger whole.

The history of America has been one of a tug of war between these two competing values. At times, we pull harder on private property rights, limited government, and low taxes. Other times, big concerns push us to broaden government's role, increase taxes, and sacrifice our individual preferences in order to serve a broader goal. The political divisiveness in Washington, DC, today is often between these competing values.

Many Democratic leaders advocate a bigger government role because of our country's needs but forget to consider the rugged individualism that is in our core. Republican leaders by and large emphasize the rights of the individual and advocate small government but forget that Americans always see themselves as part of a community. While each side is well intentioned, they miss the opportunity to find the balance in this paradox of values. This balance is what is missing today in America. We need leaders who have a big vision involving community but who can also understand that the best way to implement their agenda locally is through individuals and smaller groups of citizens.

As I drove into the Davis Mountains State Park at dusk, the sun was just kissing the mountains goodnight. I pulled up to Indian Lodge, which sits serenely on the side of one of the mountains. The Lodge was built in 1933 as part of Franklin Roosevelt's Civilian Conservation Corps (CCC). It still stands in its peaceful beauty and is used by folks venturing out into the unsettled area of west Texas.

The young men who were part of the CCC in the 1930s were sent to build a lodge in the middle of nowhere. They lived in tents, worked hard in the tough weather, and earned a little money in the midst of the Great Depression (nearly all of which they sent home to their families). It took some tough, rugged individuals to join this group. They were able to build something that has lasted for generations. Most importantly, their work gave them a bit of respect. The entirety of the CCC built respect through its projects in one of the toughest times we as a country have faced.

A few miles up the road from the Lodge is Fort Davis. This was a fort established on the frontier in the 1850s to protect folks who were traveling from San Antonio to El Paso on their way to California to seek their fortune and a better life. Harsh conditions faced these men and women as they built a life out of the desert and rocks that surrounded Fort Davis.

The residents of Fort Davis made this their home in order to protect the travelers whom they didn't even know. In fact, some of the first soldiers to occupy this remote post were the famous Buffalo Soldiers—a regiment of African Americans who helped to show other folks that color doesn't have anything to do with ability.

In each of these instances, individual Americans came together in the rawness of the Texas mountains to help build a better life not just for themselves but also for their communities and the country. These simple folks didn't complicate the endeavor with discussions about the role of government or individual rights. They bought into a broader vision. They just did what was necessary in their locale. They held the balance of the paradox of these American values.

The day after Christmas, I rose early, before the sun winked its first light, and went down to the Lodge offices to have some tea. I brought my cup and a tea bag, because the night before the park staff had said they would have hot water ready. Around five thirty a.m. in pitch dark in this remote location, I walked into the Lodge front entrance and was greeted by two women. They were so friendly and helpful.

I realized during the days I was there that most of the park's staff were women. They impressed me with their courage and strength as individuals to help other folks in this desolate but beautiful spot. Their stories were modern versions of the CCC or the settlers of Fort Davis. With tremendous courage, they had come here for a bright opportunity. They were making personal sacrifices in order to build a sense of community by helping others.

Today in America, we are looking for leaders to emerge who can speak to this paradox of values. Each of us wants to act out our individualism while also being a part of something bigger. We want to be self-reliant pioneers, pushing forward into the unknown of our destinies, but we also want to know that someone has our backs. That when we come in at night, a campfire is lit, and someone is there to greet us.

Leaders should push new and engaging ways of bringing together strong individuals who can build community projects that we can feel, see, and touch and that leave a legacy for generations to come. This isn't a new idea—it was done in the 1800s and the 1900s—but in our bitter political divide, many of our leaders have forgotten this important part of our American spirit.

We each can be pioneers in our own right. We simply have to find that balance between our rugged individual sides and our senses of family, community, and fellowship that engenders in us belonging. This is where we can recapture the true sense of American exceptionalism. Finding that balance is about threading the needle through the eye of a beautiful American paradox.

All this must start with a commitment to an overarching big vision coupled with a localized tactical strategy. Whether you are a president, a CEO, a head of a foundation, or the head of your household, you can't even begin to be successful without a vision that is big enough and encompassing enough to connect with the hearts and minds of all citizens.

There is a great line in a television series I love (*Lonesome Dove*). At the end of the series, after having gone through both wonderful success and terrible tragedy, protagonist Woodrow Call is asked by a newspaper reporter: "They say you are a man of vision. Is that true?" Woodrow reflects for a moment and then says, "Yeah, hell of a vision." It is up to our leaders to come up with their own "hell of a vision."

This big vision articulated clearly by the leader of any group or organization has to be tied to set of shared values rooted deeply both in the individual and in the team of people. The big vision must have a purpose that prompts each member to step outside of themself and into the broader goal. The vision needs to be both timeless and timely. It must fit with the time you are in and be cognizant of where in the present moment you might be as president of a company or president of the country. It also must be a vision that can stretch across time, reaching into future generations for years to come.

Yes, a leader can be successful in the short term with only a temporary goal and a strategy that fits the current balance sheet. However, you won't achieve purposeful or meaningful impact with a vision too small. You will satisfy only the appetites of the present moment.

I have counseled many candidates—from leaders of small businesses to the leader of the free world—that leaders with real impact started with a big vision. This vision isn't fundamentally about strategy, tactics, personal ambition, or financial gain. It must be other-focused, not self-involved. And it must totally root itself in, and become an integral part of, the culture of the organization. It isn't just a slogan, but it still needs to be simple enough to feel, see, and touch. We each—in whatever capacity we serve as leaders—must decide what our dreams are for and translate this decision into a vision. Once this is done, it is time to move on to tactics.

Tactically today: We heed the call of the small. To put it snappily, the local is the focal.

A few years ago, my friend Nicco Mele wrote an excellent book titled *The End of Big*. He posits that as technology has accelerated, people's lives have drastically changed. We have lost faith and trust in institution after institution. Success for leaders will no longer be achieved in massive, hierarchical organizations but in their capturing a smaller place in this larger world. This disruption will include businesses, churches, schools, philanthropy, politics, and government. And the public wholeheartedly agrees.

In poll after poll, we see that the American public trusts smaller and more locally based institutions and government far more than those that are larger and more distant from where voters live and work. The American public sees the small and local as better equipped to do their missions effectively and act in their best interests.

Small business, local government, and local media are seen in a significantly better light than their larger and more distant counterparts. Citizens across partisan lines believe that the local institutions will consistently act on their behalf. The federal government, large corporations, the United States Congress, President Trump, the national parties, and the national media are seen at best as mediocre and at worst as disconnected from representing and serving the interests of average voters.

Interestingly, when we look back in history, we can recall that the most profound change and leadership emerged from our local communities and neighborhoods.

This is also true today. Leaders who speak the truth and serve compassionately among our locales are the ones who have fundamentally changed the world.

Jesus lived and traveled his entire life in an area smaller than most cities of today. Buddha taught and acted in a very tiny regional area. Muhammad lived and spoke in the sands and tents of his community. Saint Francis of Assisi rebuilt an entire church and showed the world a new way to act while living his entire life in a geographic span smaller than most of today's neighborhoods. It wasn't the tactics employed by television, radio, the Internet, or public relations and advertising professionals that made them powerful agents of change in the world. It was the power of the truth they spoke and their local actions that changed people's lives.

Leaders of today can learn both from local citizens and from the lessons of leaders from the past that authentic change is trusted and desired in smaller ways in our communities. We need to relearn the lesson that if leaders want to be successful and build genuine trust and connection among the public, they must operate and engage locally.

The political parties would be smart, when designing policy and solutions for our needs, to recognize that voters don't necessarily want a distant, disengaged federal program. Both political parties seem stuck in a broken reaction. Many Republicans oppose government initiatives but lean on large corporations as being credible. Many Democrats recognize the need for government intervention but too reflexively push national government–based solutions. Neither party is speaking for where the country desires to go.

Small, local businesses are seen as best representing our interests, but businesses continue to consolidate and grow larger, further disconnecting themselves from average folks. I understand that cost savings and critical mass can be had by centralizing operations into larger entities, but what good is it for the business if it means it loses the faith and trust of its consumers?

Future leaders must design new models that serve and relate more locally. Leaders need to be creative in building and extending operations and responses out of the boardrooms of Wall Street and out of the halls of power in Washington, DC. One of the best ways to overcome the lack of faith and polarization we feel in our old leadership models is to adopt a more local method.

This method must include our churches and educational institutions, which for too long have been set up on a centralized model of hierarchical command and control, where their dream seems to be "bigger is better." As these institutions have grown bigger, not only have they become disconnected from their original visions, but they have also lost touch with their constituents.

When we look at the generational breakdown, we see that younger voters are demanding big visions accompanied by local action to an even greater degree. The success of locally led social entrepreneurs is the harbinger of what most young people are hungry for. This movement is growing in Austin, Wimberley, Detroit, New York City, Boston, and every town, small and large, across America. It is time for leaders in business and in Washington to recognize that the old structures aren't trusted and don't effectively serve the interests of most Americans.

A recent example of this new model is how quickly the "Country over Party" logo came to be on T-shirts available to folks around the country. I was having lunch one day with two friends, Adam and Marty Butler, who founded an agency in Austin, the Butler Brothers, to help companies in the marketplace. I was talking about the need for leaders to put country over party. They immediately said, "That would make a great logo," and then, to my surprise and pleasure, they had their company design one.

Within days, they had a compelling logo done as part of their contribution to the effort. Days later, a company in Austin, Fort Lonesome studio, which does amazing cross-stitching, volunteered to stitch a "Country-over-Party" banner. When they were done with the banner, a local photographer offered to take some pictures of the banner and me by my truck out in a field. I posted that picture online. Within a couple of hours, a startup company in Pittsburgh, Cotton Bureau, said they would love to crowdsource T-shirts. They had a mocked-up T-shirt with the "Country-over-Party" logo on the web in ninety minutes.

The shirt sold nearly four hundred in two weeks. Amazing change happening locally and organically.

We see again that voters in this country, even if not sophisticated, are ahead of most national leaders on what works best in their lives. As I have always said, national leaders don't lead, they follow where the country is already signaling it wants to go. The best leaders figure that out and then try to get one step in front of the direction the country is already moving in.

I climbed the ladder of perceived success all the way to the White House and became an expert at modern communication tactics before I *finally* realized that the most enormous impact we can make is in our local communities, families, and relationships. It took my walking in the traditional halls of power of business and government to rediscover where real power is—in the small circles of my life.

Yes, leaders assuredly must begin with a big, robust, values-laden vision and create a culture that reflects this. But then they must push out the implementation locally and through small circles where trust remains solid. The exceptional leaders of today and tomorrow will understand that leadership in the paradox of big vision and local action will be part of the new way.

CHAPTER EIGHT

IDEALISM/REALISM

Every leader is typically forced into a choice between the path of idealism versus the path of realism. We are often told we have to choose to look at life *idealistically* or be in life *realistically*. Idealists are told to get their heads out of the clouds, come down to earth, and be "real." Realists are told to dream bigger, to not accept what is, and to act from a place of higher ideals.

We see this paradox operate in our personal lives as well as in the lives of leaders in politics, business, and philanthropy. However, the greatest leaders of our time will be those who can hold the paradox of both idealism and realism.

One of the first steps of standing in that paradox—and one of the hardest things to do in our lives—is to let go of what we want to happen or think should happen in order to see clearly what *is* happening.

So many times in my own life, I have found it very difficult to hold simultaneously the paradox of my idealism about what was in front of me while looking clearly as a realist at what was actually going on. This difficulty begets paralysis and causes us terrible trouble. For example, that paralysis is why we get into, or stay in, dysfunctional relationships for far too long. We so badly want to believe what we want our partner to be that we can't look through the fog of our optimistic (or deluded) heart.

We suffer long in endeavors and with people we shouldn't. We can't accept that our initial judgment might have been wrong, that it was based on what we wanted it to be as opposed to what is intolerable. It is easier for us to make judgments based on what we think someone should be or how we want something to turn out than it is to lay the *shoulds* and *wants* temporarily down to be able to see with clear eyes what is happening directly in front of us. It is why the first step in every addiction program is to admit the truth.

And this same misadventure occurs often in politics, especially among the media and campaign operatives who have a strong storyline of what they would like to happen. We might not like a certain candidate, so we judge everything as problematic or damaging about them when that actually may not be what is occurring. We like or want a certain candidate to win, so we judge events through that prism and we misread problems ahead. In psychological parlance, this is called *denial*. I describe it as when we confuse our wants with what actually is.

This denial just happened in the recent presidential election, where many of us misread what was happening in the Midwestern states and were shocked when Trump won the Electoral College vote. Not only did folks in the media have it wrong, but folks in the Trump campaign and the Clinton campaign were also shocked by the result. This isn't the first time this has happened in the modern era. Many GOP pundits (and Romney staffers) predicted a Mitt Romney victory in 2012, even though all available data pointed to a big victory for President Obama. They wanted Romney to win, so they couldn't see the data right in front of them. The same was true in 2004, when Democrats convinced themselves Kerry would win when all the data indicated a Bush victory ahead.

So many observers of Trump and Clinton have operated from this "should" vantage point. The GOP establishment took far too long to even accept that Trump would be the nominee, because they couldn't read the signs. Their "should" got in the way. Democrats supporting Hillary were also in denial, not accepting her vulnerability and the warning signals ahead in the general election period. Even with Jeb Bush, people had so considered the money he had raised as significant that they thought he was dominant. They had a hard time seeing that this storyline was a bit of a myth.

The media starts from an assumption that what has always happened will keep happening—that money still matters a huge amount, that policy positions decide elections, that people vote with their heads rather than their hearts, and that, in the end, each party will nominate the heir apparent in the process. In the 2016 election, they neglected to see that right in front of them was an electorate who desired disruption of the status quo, an electorate who wanted something very different from the duopoly partisan state.

My fear is that the advent of Trump will soon be the occasion of a misreading by the media and operatives from both sides of the aisle of what is going on in America. Because they want the rules of engagement and the norms in politics to be right, they will misread the lessons of the Trump victory and the Clinton loss. They will look at either result from a prism of what their original story was instead of what actually happened.

Did Trump's personality, tone, and manner set him apart from the other candidates and contribute a bit to his victory? Yes—however, Trump won in spite of himself, not because of himself. Trump was elected on Election Day with the highest unfavorability rating of anyone to win, and he entered office with the highest disapproval rating of any incoming president. A major portion of Trump's vote was not pro-Trump but anti-Clinton. In the end, a few thousand voters in a few states preferred a distrusted outsider rather than a distrusted insider.

Additionally, the two legacy parties need to look long and hard at themselves. Neither one represents the whole of America. Republicans hold most of the offices today, but they have a huge demographic problem, because the fastest-growing parts of the electorate are against them. Democrats have a huge geographic problem, where most states, counties, and other political jurisdictions are voting consistently against their party's candidates. In order for political leaders to see reality, they need to look at America with eyes wide open.

The status quo has forever changed. If we set down our "shoulds" and our "wants," we will begin to see that truth. Only then can we make the right decisions going forward on what to do and understand what Americans really want. We need leaders who can blend the right combination of idealism and realism. Who hold a positive, optimistic, hopeful, unifying, values-driven vision in their hearts while approaching our country and the world with clear eyes.

We have seen presidents throughout our history default into idealism and get themselves and our country in trouble. John F. Kennedy learned from his mistake of being too idealistic from the Bay of Pigs incident. Then, having learned his lesson, he handled the Cuban Missile Crisis with a combination of idealism and realism. President Bush's entry into the Iraq War was a tragic example of putting ideals ahead of realism, and the country is still suffering from our inability to find the balance.

I am hoping President Trump approaches our foreign policy with a combination of realism and idealism. We want to convey our ideals across the globe: human rights, democracy, security, tolerance, and acceptance. We need to have policies articulated that are rooted in these deeply held ideals. Let us remember that the Declaration of Independence states that all people are "endowed by their Creator with certain unalienable Rights, that among these are Life, Liberty and the pursuit of Happiness." But we also want our leaders to be realistic about the partners, allies, and actions that we might have to take in order to enforce those ideals and our own security around the globe.

A problem can develop not only from being too idealistic but also from adopting an overly realistic "ends justify the means" approach to leadership. The idea of ends justifying the means has been attributed to Machiavelli, who lived five centuries ago, and it has been followed too diligently by leaders in politics and business ever since. We need to get past that old model.

One day in November 2010, as I was sitting on my back porch listening to the Blanco River splashing over the stones and the wind gently moving through the live oaks, I heard a ping on my iPhone. Looking down, I noticed an email from an assistant to President Barack Obama at the White House, asking if I could have a meeting with the president at the beginning of December. The president and his party had suffered terrible losses in the midterm election, so I figured he was reaching out in some way for advice and what next steps I might suggest. I said sure, and I started to think about the one piece of advice I would give him.

I had worked on Democratic campaigns starting with my freshman year in college in St. Louis. I got out of politics for a bit in the 1990s, after helping Democrat Bob Bullock get elected and reelected as Texas lieutenant governor. In 1994, Bullock won reelection at the same time that George W. Bush won the governor's race. Like many in Texas, I became a fan of Governor Bush and his bipartisanship. I ended up working on his presidential race in 2000, and I served as his chief strategist in 2004, before later having a public break with him.

In October 2006, then-Senator Obama reached out to have that breakfast meeting at the Driskill Hotel in Austin. (Actually it was his press adviser, Robert Gibbs, who would later become Obama's White House press secretary, with whom I had become good friends, who reached out to me.) Senator Obama and I met for about an hour—both with our feet up on a table outside the restaurant at the hotel. He talked about ending the bitterness in Washington, DC, and about bringing people together. This was very similar to the rationale behind President Bush's run for president in 2000.

I gave Senator Obama some thoughts on his running for president (he had not yet formally decided, but you could tell he was moving in that direction). He actually asked for my opinions about his running, though I think he had pretty much decided. I said I thought this race against Hillary Clinton would be tough, but you never know when another window will open again, if ever. People pass up opportunities all the time, hoping for something in the future, but they may never get that chance again.

I was very impressed with his smarts, calm demeanor, and vision for the world ahead. In fact, I voted for him in 2008, primarily because I thought he could change the polarized politics in Washington. (I ended up *not* voting for him in 2012, because the country had become more polarized while he was president.) Once he was elected, not surprisingly, I didn't talk to him again until the White House reached out in late 2010. Once people get elected to the office of president, it is unfortunately very difficult for them to maintain relationships with folks outside their very inner circle.

In December 2010, on a cold day in Washington, I walked in the back entrance of the White House and prepared to meet with President Obama. So many thoughts were swirling in my mind. It is a heady experience to visit the White House. Even though I had been there numerous times before at meetings throughout the Bush presidency, I always felt a bit of awe.

I wasn't nervous or intimidated, though. I was raised by a mom who constantly pushed the idea that no one is better than you—and that you are better than no one. No matter how much money, celebrity status, or power someone has, they are no more special than you. It is something I have carried with me throughout my life, sometimes maybe as a little burr under my saddle.

As I walked through the staff offices in the West Wing, I got the feeling that many of them were wondering what a former strategist to President Bush was doing here. I definitely was under the impression that this was a meeting the president had set up outside of staff consultation, which is never a good thing for the guest.

I entered the Oval Office, shook hands with President Obama, and sat down. It was just the two of us: no staff, no assistants, no operatives. In meetings with presidents, these are highly unusual circumstances, and I was impressed. In fact, having worked for President Bush for five years, I had never once had a one-on-one meeting with him.

President Obama's hair had grayed considerably since I had seen him last, and he was much thinner. This happens to most presidents. We caught up on family and pleasantries, and I mentioned to him that he had lost weight since I saw him last. This is understandable, knowing the stresses of the office. He said he had started drinking two shakes a day to keep the weight on. We then turned to the purpose of his reaching out.

"What do you think went wrong in the first two years?" he asked me.

"Let's not rehash the past," I said, knowing that he realized the mistakes and missteps. "Let's talk about moving forward." Often we so get caught up looking in the rearview mirror that we forget where we are going. It is good to understand the past, but at some point we have to move on and take steps into the future.

We talked about a lot of things, policies, and people. About dealing with Congress and being more open. I even mentioned a thought I'd had about doing some large-scale national service effort, so that young people, now so disappointed and disconnected, could feel a part of something bigger than themselves. I said he needed some new American Peace Corps that was his own. He nodded at times and argued at others. President Obama is a smart guy, but sometimes he wants to prove too much how smart he is.

And I said while all that was important, I had one big point to make. It was very similar to what I had mentioned to him at the Driskill Hotel in 2006.

I said that he needed to concentrate more on the means of governing and less on the ends. That the American public had become even more frustrated because the federal government wasn't working and was incredibly dysfunctional. That in order for the public to accept the ends of policy, they needed to believe that the means were good.

A major problem with the healthcare reform he had passed was that it had been done in a very divisive and polarizing way. He had little to no Republican support.

Moving on the bill without that support would sow the seeds of damage in the months and years ahead. The policy of healthcare reform and winning the fight had become more important than the manner in which it was done. As I write this now, I am afraid President Trump and the GOP Congress are headed toward doing the same thing on healthcare reform.

The old maxim that the ends justify the means must be turned completely around. The means justify the ends. How we behave, what our communications are like, how we engage with people in relationships, and the process of governing and coming together in discussion are far more important than the ends. This is what most spiritual leaders throughout history have taught. Don't worry about the afterlife, concentrate on today and on your life's journey in this moment. If you do that well, the ends will take care of themselves.

If we are able to improve the means of our interactions with people, with nature, with business, and with governing, then we can trust the ends. We can trust that what comes out of that will be good. That if we change the discourse and unmoor ourselves from the anchors of our desired ends, if we just focus on improving the process, the country will be much better off. Then the public will once again regain the faith in the governmental institutions that they have almost completely lost trust in.

President Obama and I had a long discussion about this,

and he seemed to agree. We parted ways, and I walked out on the front lawn of the White House with a smile on my face. He said he wanted to do this again, maybe once every six to eight weeks. He said he had felt too cocooned and wasn't getting enough diverse advice. I told him that I was game for it and even though I had become disappointed in his leadership, that I was happy to help for the sake of the country. However, I told him that I didn't expect we would meet anytime soon, because his staff would not let this kind of meeting happen again. He said, "I am the president and can meet with whomever I like." We never met again.

I had some hope that maybe he and his administration would try to concentrate on the means as opposed to the ends, even though it seems much easier to default to the old politics and the polarized discussions. Unfortunately, in the end, the Obama administration defaulted back to the old way of ends justifying means. And I am now very worried about the Trump administration. They justify any means to achieve victory. Each time they are held accountable, they say, "We won." As if winning justifies any tactics or behavior.

I did smile as I walked out of the White House after meeting with President Obama, crossing the front lawn and through the security gate, thinking that this boy from Detroit was a long way from delivering newspapers after school. I thought that the idea of the means justifying the ends is really how I needed more and more to live my life. That I might not be able to change the manner in which an administration could operate, but I could certainly do better on this account in my own world. As we each can.

In the intimate relationships of my own life, I have the power to work on the means and to let the ends come as they should. If leaders could focus on the means, we would then be better able to hold the paradox of idealism and realism in balance. Defaulting into one or the other may give us the comfort of our own assuredness, but it doesn't help lead our communities forward.

CHAPTER NINE

BOUNDARIES/ OPENNESS

Each of us struggles in our lives both to maintain boundaries that protect us and to be open to the influence of others as they help us grow. We are frequently given conflicting advice that seems to pull us in opposite directions. We are instructed to make sure we have solid boundaries in our lives and relationships. We are told we need to have strong boundaries to protect us from a world we cannot trust. But then we are encouraged to be open and transparent to the world as it is. We are told the only avenue to growth is through knocking down boundaries and living life open to all that the world has to offer.

Ah, yes, another paradox we are going to have to find the balance in. This one has taken me quite a long time to understand; I have suffered hurt and pain from too many boundaries and also from too much openness. Our country too has experienced similar suffering. Either our boundaries (and I don't mean walls) weren't built solidly enough by our leaders, or our leaders didn't trust the public and weren't open or transparent enough to allow this great democracy to grow.

As you can probably guess by now, I am a hopeful romantic and a big fan of sappy movies, especially Christmas stories. "Well, in Whoville they say that the Grinch's small heart grew three sizes that day. And then the true meaning of Christmas came through, and the Grinch found the strength of ten Grinches, plus two!" And thus, the redemption story of *How the Grinch Stole Christmas* is resolved. His old self dies and a new self is born, one created out of generosity and love.

For many years growing up, I thought I was going to die young. For some reason, I had determined I would die by the time I was forty-five or so. I don't know where this came from, but it settled into my psyche, and I became convinced it was going to happen. This sense of urgency combined with my natural ambition meant that I was always in a hurry. I also wasn't that concerned with others' feelings, being much more concerned with my own.

When I turned forty-five, I thought I had made it past the barrier of living. The "dying young" story of my youth apparently wasn't true. It was like I had been freed. I had a whole new life to live. Then, within a few months, my mom was found dead on the living room floor of our Michigan home. She had just gotten my younger brother out of the house—the baby of the eleven of us (he had recently turned eighteen). Mom died of a heart attack shortly after the home was empty for the first time in thirty-eight years. It shocked all of us and turned my father's world upside down. None of us had dealt with death in this kind of close manner before.

It made me pause for a bit, but not long enough for me to rest in the moment and reflect on how I might make my life different. Then, not too many years later, my wife at the time and I tragically lost a daughter. She was an identical twin, and her sister, who is a beautiful young woman today, was in the hospital for nine months.

My daughter's passing was followed by our oldest son enlisting in the army. He was sent on two dangerous tours in Iraq. And then not long after, my older brother called and told me that my younger sister had been found dead in her apartment from an accidental drug overdose.

Okay, now God or the universe had my attention. Each loss was wrenching in its own way. When you lose a parent, you are losing your guardian. Losing a sibling is like losing one of your own, a partner. And losing a child is something you never expect to happen. It took all of those things to crack me. It was now really the time to reflect and determine how I wanted to live my life. It took many years of contemplation, prayer, heartache, and trial and error, but I came out the other side.

I think there are two paths people can take when they suffer loss or terrible pain. On one path, your heart can get smaller. You can close off. You can get more cynical, become more self-focused, and treat others with less compassion. On the other path, you can become more hopeful and optimistic, more open. You can become less self-centered and more loving. Your heart can grow bigger. You can break down some of the artificial boundaries you have erected and live life more connected and transparent.

Because of faith (and maybe some courage), I was able to take the latter path. I reentered the world with a sense of courage and faith. These qualities were molded on my pilgrimage. As with the Grinch, I like to believe my heart grew more in size in the aftermath of all that heartbreak.

I made discoveries on the path to openness mixed with secure boundaries. For example, I realized that for a long time, I had wanted to be a nice person, but I probably wasn't always kind. Recently, someone had told me I was a nice guy. I replied, "No, I am not—I want to be kind." There is a huge difference between the two.

Being nice refers to how we want to be perceived by others. What we do to make others see us in a certain way. Being kind, however, is an inherent, rooted value that speaks to who we are and how we convey that in the world. Being nice is an external disposition. Being kind is an internal disposition. When we are kind, we go out into the world in a loving manner simply because that is who we are. "Nice" is getting people to like us because of what we do. "Kind" is treating others in the way our hearts and souls naturally gravitate to, since they are rooted in that deep value.

Though polite and gracious, I am not always a nice person. I sometimes say truths that upset others, or I don't care what someone really thinks of me. If I know for myself who I really am, based on my rooted values, it is okay for folks to say I am not nice, as long as I know I am being kind. I am kind to myself with boundaries, so that I protect myself and maintain my way. I am kind to others without seeking a return from them. I try to be as open and transparent as possible.

As I look for the leaders of our country and our communities, I am not looking for nice people, but for kind people. Leaders who are strong enough to have gone through tragedy and come out the other side more open, compassionate, and loving.

There are many leaders who are nice to people, but their niceness is rooted in trying to get something in return. They smile, but they don't respect others. They are using political or economic institutions for self-aggrandizement or personal gain. They think success is about "winning," but really success is about *being*. And a huge part of real success is being kind—openly but with boundaries that ground you. This is part of our new way of leadership and living. Our leaders must translate this institutionally into politics, government, and business.

So how does a leader do this in practice? How would a president or a CEO approach this paradox of boundary and openness?

WikiLeaks has been a major story in the news over the past few years. They are an organization whose guiding principle claims to be transparency in all things: openness to all information, regardless of the manner it is obtained. During this past election, they selectively released private and stolen information, likely gathered by the Russian government, which hurt Hillary Clinton in her presidential campaign. Many believe their leaks were a factor in her loss and actively undermined our democracy.

I stated at the time that I didn't know how anyone could applaud their actions, since it was private information (not governmental) that was leaked, and the sole purpose of the leak was to hurt one candidate in a partisan way and help another at the behest of a foreign government. Interestingly, Democratic leaders roundly condemned the WikiLeaks release, while most Republicans either celebrated it or remained quiet and just allowed it to do its damage.

A few years ago, I had written a column applauding WikiLeaks for their transparency when Republicans and Democrats almost universally condemned the intrusion into "government" secrets (one principle they seem to agree on is protecting "government's privacy"). The column read in part:

As I was sitting with my three sons over the post-Thanksgiving weekend, watching football at their place (where they have lived together for nearly a year without any major fight, or the police showing up, or burning the place down), my oldest son, who served in the army for five years and was deployed in Iraq for nearly a year and a half, turned to me and asked, "When as a country did we become a place where the government gets upset when their secrets are revealed, but they have no problem knowing all our secrets and invading our privacy?"

Hmm... interesting question.

In the polarized environment and existing bitter rhetoric in Washington, DC, ironically there is bipartisan agreement on a couple things. Both parties agree that the government has a right to listen in on all our phone conversations and read emails with very little evidence needed in the name of national security. Both parties believe that any information the government decides is in the national interest and is classified can be withheld from the public for as long as it wants. Both parties agree that when someone reveals this information they should be universally condemned while the press corps stays mute.

I recall during the Clinton administration when Republicans expressed outrage over the healthcare taskforce holding "secret" meetings and not releasing attendees and discussion.

Then, not many years later, Democrats expressed similar outrage at the secrecy of the Bush administration holding meetings related to energy policy. Now both sides have gotten together to attack WikiLeaks over the exact opposite problem—openly releasing information to the public of discussion related to foreign policy.

Everyone in Washington, DC, claims support for transparency and openness of the government during campaign season and public posturing. They castigate the other side when they do things in secret, saying that the proceedings must be nefarious if the information is withheld. But then, when it comes to the recent disclosures, we hear folks at all levels saying that release of this information will endanger lives, that it is a threat to national security, or that the founder of WikiLeaks is a criminal.

When did we arrive as a culture where we trust the government more to keep secrets than the citizenry? When is revealing the truth about what the government is doing a negative thing? And why is the media complicit in this? Did we not learn anything in the run-up to the war in Iraq when hard questions weren't asked and we accepted statements from government officials without proper pushback?

My own sense is that we should err on the side of telling the truth even when it is inconvenient in our own lives or in what the government is doing. People who tell the truth should, at the very least, not be denigrated. This is something I learned when I was young and have tried to impart to my three boys as they grew up. As Albert Einstein said: "The search for truth implies a duty. One must not conceal any part of what one has recognized to be true."

And shouldn't the press be defending WikiLeaks? Shouldn't they actually be doing some soul searching of their own to discover why they aren't devoting more resources to the search for the truth? Why do outlets like the *National Enquirer* and blogs on the Internet seem better at discovering the truth than these huge national media organizations?

When we have a federal government widely distrusted by the public, maybe we can all reflect a bit on what a former young soldier, who put himself in harm's way defending freedom, our way of life, and the Constitution (including the First Amendment), asked me in a living room in Austin during a football game?

"When as a country did we become a place where the government gets upset when their secrets are revealed, but they have no problem knowing all our secrets and invading our privacy? If we want to restore trust in our government, maybe we could start with being given the truth, with the government keeping less secrets and respecting the privacy of average citizens."

I still stand by nearly all of what I wrote in 2010, but as I have tried to be in the paradox of transparency and boundaries, I also advocate a more nuanced approach. Transparency and openness are essential. But, just as important, we must also ensure there are boundaries surrounding private communications that are hacked solely for the purpose of affecting an election.

Leaders in Washington and around the country in politics and business, journalists and the media, even presidents, must be able to maintain that balance. Our default position should be that the government can trust citizens with most information as long it is isn't in the real national security interest of the country to hold back that information. And, from my read, most information can be released by the government without compromising our national security.

The test is, is information being withheld to protect the country or to protect your position? For example, the Pentagon Papers were classified for a long time. When they were finally released, not much in them represented a threat to our national security. So why had they been classified? I believe it was an act of self-interest rather than national interest.

This paradigm applies as well to business leaders, who should operate with openness and transparency—unless there is a broader community value, which would require a boundary on information. Not a profit or preservation motive, but community-driven importance.

Conversely, average Americans and all leaders should expect a boundary surrounding private communication and a zone of privacy around their lives—unless there is a community purpose that demands the release of private information, especially if that information had been obtained illegally. And that requires a tough decision by someone coming from an authentic place.

The private lives and discussions of leaders of all institutions should be off-limits unless those communications have direct community impact. Breaking those boundaries to win an election, move up the corporate ladder, or achieve some level of power, success, or partisan advantage in the world are not good enough reasons.

Secrets are a dangerous thing to keep, but so is breaking a secret for a self-serving purpose. What happens in our relationships when we either keep secrets for the wrong reason or break them for the wrong reasons? It usually means that our relationships don't have trust and are doomed to either fail or lose their security, freedom, and closeness. We have seen a total breakdown of trust in our government, corporations, the Catholic Church, and media institutions when they have lost their way in this paradox. When they kept secrets that should not have been kept but didn't honor privacy when the situation demanded it.

Just as in a personal relationship, leaders function in a relationship with their communities of interest—customers, citizens, or clients. Good relationships are built on mutual trust. We should begin with the premise that sharing information and being open is a good thing for our country and our relationships—but protecting one another is just as key. Balancing those two competing principles is a crucial component in leading in a new way.

CHAPTER TEN

DELEGATION/
ACCOUNTABILITY

America recently elected a businessman billionaire as president of the United States. Many citizens believed that applying the practices of business to government would help resolve dysfunction, making bureaucratic operations more effective and efficient. I would suggest the two principles we most desperately need in organizations, both large and small, public and private, and at all levels, are the ability to delegate and the hunger for accountability.

In 2001, there were expectations that the new president (whom I worked for) would run the executive branch with his business expertise. President Bush was the first occupant of the White House to hold an MBA. Due to the complex nature of our vast federal government and the very complicated world we live in, many people thought he would put these two business principles—delegation and accountability—into practice.

President Bush had watched his father serve as president for four years, and he himself had been the governor of Texas, the second largest state in the union. He was well aware that leading was not a one-person job. With an extended federal workforce, layers of management, and huge budgets for every agency, he understood the need for and benefit of delegation in the running of the White House.

In 2009, President Obama took office without much experience in management and no experience in business. But he had tremendous experience in building coalitions as a legislator and organizing with others in communities to bring about change. He, too, had learned through his life experience that it takes many people to accomplish a goal. His broad campaign slogan was "Yes, We Can."

President Obama was very well practiced in the art of delegation but not so much in the just-as-important principle of proper accountability. As with President Bush, this weakness was apparent as he delegated daily but didn't use accountability as much as the country needed. Numerous cabinet officials were delegated responsibility, but they were not held accountable.

I have noticed the same pattern appear while consulting with CEOs in business and philanthropy, serving on the boards of charitable organizations, or taking part in social entrepreneurship. So many leaders are good at delegation (giving power and tasks away to others) so that the work can get done as a whole, but very few leaders are good at accountability. Accountability in conjunction with delegation seems a lost art. We need both MBA 101 (Delegation) and MBA 201 (Accountability).

It became known in family lore as "the Trial." Whenever we adults gather as a family, it is one of the stories that is often repeated and held out as a classic Dowd story. Well, "classic" in the Dowd dysfunctional mythology anyway. One of my brothers still feels like it was some show trial or kangaroo court, where justice was railroaded through. He just brought it up again the other day, partly in jest but also very serious. Moments in time really do live on and on.

Late one summer afternoon, one of my younger brothers (Dan) decided he was a little bored and that he needed to pass the time by playing with fire (literally, not figuratively). As with early man, fire has been a huge part of the younger male tradition in our family. We might play games involving kicking or throwing lit balls of fire, or lighting fires in a field just to watch what happens, or collecting unused fireworks from a high school stadium and lighting them off again without knowing exactly where they may end up. Collecting matches or lighters became a version of our own hoarding. Playing with fire was passed on from one to the other over the course of the years, and it was embraced by each as a crucial part of the adventure of childhood.

My mom and pop had five sons born in a row in the 1960s—Pat, Matt, Mike, Paul, and Dan. (The oldest in our family of eleven is Mary Denise, who, interestingly, is an emergency room pediatrician. She deals daily with injuries among children, including injuries from fire.) Dan was a small, scrappy kid.

He got the brunt in the push and pull of sibling dynamics. He really had to fight to survive in that mix. Later in life, he joined the marines and was an embassy guard in Panama and Kuwait right before each invasion in those countries. Seems as though his youth had prepared him for his next phase—or had determined his next one. A psychologist or an astrologer will have to figure out which.

So on that summer day, Dan, who was around seven or eight at the time, knew that the key ingredients to "fire play" were matches and gasoline. Because my pop had caught onto us a while back, and—no idiot him—he had begun hiding the gasoline cans or putting them way out of our reach on a shelf in the garage. But Dan was onto that (as we all were). He knew there was gasoline in the tank of the lawn mower. That, combined with the matches he had saved over time, meant he had what he needed.

He wheeled the lawn mower out to the front lawn behind some trees, grabbed a small stick, and started to play. Being a bit young, he didn't know all the nuances of this operation, so he decided to just dip the stick in the lawn mower's gas tank, hold it out, light the wet end, and wave it around. He was having good fun, until in one quick moment, the fire got too close to his fingers. He immediately dropped the stick.

He watched in slow motion as the stick fell straight into the open lawn mower tank, lighting the mower on fire, melting one glob of plastic on it, and making an incredible mess. Dan knew that he had to put out the fire and then hide the evidence. So, he wheeled the burnt lawn mower near the garden hose and doused the fire. Fortunately, this worked.

He didn't want to tell anyone what he'd done (each of us has a tendency to want to have fun but, when it gets out of control, not to suffer the consequences), so he just wheeled the mower back into the garage and nonchalantly walked into the house. None of us had any idea what had just transpired, although some of us to this day can recall a smell of gasoline as we watched television.

Well, fast-forward to the next day. My pop wanted to cut the lawn that morning. He pushed the lawn mower out to the yard and pulled the cord that starts it (remember those ancient models from years ago?). The only thing that happened was that a small bit of burnt rope broke off in his hands—just a blackened nub from the starter cord. He looked down and saw that the plastic of the mower parts were all melted together. Whatever else he was doing, he certainly wasn't cutting the lawn that morning.

Of course, my pop threw a fit. He started yelling and screaming, then accusing each of his kids. Every single one of us (including Dan) denied having done it. Pop had nowhere to go with this, so he just fumed and got madder and madder. He was about to impose punishment on all of us.

My mom reacted much more rationally, and she suggested a trial. She was always the leader in moments of insanity, providing much needed calm. Sometimes, in the midst of some craziness, she would just gather the kids around a table and teach us poker. Weirdly, we loved her suggestion. The idea of a court proceeding sounded like fun. I was totally on board and wanted a key role in the trial.

Though most people outside the family assumed she wasn't very smart, or that she was unsophisticated and uneducated because of all the kids she had, Mom was actually very well read. She was as smart as anyone, having graduated with highest honors from the Jesuit school, the University of Detroit. She appointed herself judge in the trial.

I was made prosecutor by the judge—a role I embraced with vigor and enthusiasm. One of my other brothers was the defense attorney for the accused. The court was set up in our family room with chairs and tables. The likely suspect list was narrowed down to three people—Dan, Paul, and Katie. Maybe most of us had airtight alibis or had been with my mom and pop at the suspected time—I don't know.

I proceeded to present evidence in front of my mom as

the judge. I cross-examined each of the accused. They were well represented by the defense attorney. We narrowed the list down to two—Dan and Katie—but weren't getting much further. I couldn't crack either one.

My mom decided to see if she could get a confession out of Dan or Katie. She took each one back to her chambers (Mom and Pop's bedroom) and had a heart-to-heart talk. With her gentle questioning, Dan broke and admitted everything. My mom came out and announced what had happened. She said she was proud of Dan for telling the truth. She also said Dan had told her that I had showed him how to get gasoline out of the tank, so I was probably accountable, too. It is probably true that Dan had seen me do this at some point. And, as I was the prosecutor, this new information completely undermined any authority I might have in some future trial.

Dan to this day thinks (or at least says it in order to engage in banter) that I had set him up. He acknowledges that he had lit the lawn mower on fire, but he believes that there was a conflict of interest in the trial. I was known to have lit fires like this before, was involved in coming up with the accused list, and was appointed prosecutor in some secret way. The judge (my mom) passed on years back, so the mystery of the trial—where blame really lay—likely went with her to her grave.

The good news, I guess, was that Dan received a very limited and just punishment—and that was the first and last trial we ever had. Each of us learned a bit about how life works and what goes on in the real world. Okay, maybe our world was just this side of crazy, but it seemed to have a structure. I learned that my mom's measured, calm way of handling things seemed like the better approach than the volatility of my pop. But can you blame him for being a little shocked as he held that burnt nub in his hand?

Accountability is a tough thing. We want other people to be accountable for their actions, but we ourselves sometimes seek to avoid or lessen the impact of a just sentence, because we believe there are extenuating circumstances for us. We want to judge others in black-and-white terms. We believe there is a definitive right and wrong. We seem to know the truth explicitly. But, for ourselves, we implore others to see the gray, to not judge us too harshly.

In looking at the art of accountability, I realize that it is as much or more about holding ourselves accountable as it is about holding others accountable. I have watched Presidents Bush and Obama find it incredibly difficult to acknowledge mistakes they made with any degree of self-accountability.

As I stated earlier in this book, both these presidents viewed admitting mistakes as a sign of weakness instead of a sign of strength. Without this admission, true account-ability would never exist in their organizations.

We now have a new president, who has taken to new levels his lack of admission of error and his inability to apologize. This lack of accountability does not bode well for a national government to work on behalf of *all* Americans.

We have seen time and time again with leaders in all communities across America that a lack of accountability costs trust. The beginning stage of accountability in any organization starts with the leaders holding themselves to a certain standard and admitting fault.

When I was younger in Michigan, I caddied at a rather exclusive country club. I learned about life for the wealthy people and the connected people who belonged to the golf club. The members were pillars in the community (businessmen and women, ministers, politicians, and wealthy retired folks). I recall overhearing at times talk about how poor folks needed to just be more accountable and responsible in their lives. Or they would talk about the sense of entitlement that existed in communities around Detroit and would say that much of this led to crime and bad behavior.

And then, in the course of caddying for some of these "country club" folks, I would watch them move the ball to a better position without their playing partners knowing. Or I would see them use what we would call a "foot wedge" to kick their ball away from a tree. Some would cheat throughout the round of golf while simultaneously talking about the lack of accountability in society. Though this behavior didn't diminish my love for the game of golf, it sure gave me a lesson in hypocrisy.

That's because, in professional golf, the participants are actually obligated to call penalties on themselves. This is unlike every other sport. If something happens in the course of play and the other players don't see it, the players are responsible for penalizing themselves. I have watched this happen among pro players, where hundreds of thousands of dollars are on the line. I've seen it among amateurs, where only a few beers and bragging rights are at play. It is the ultimate in self-accountability, of taking responsibility for your own actions and for what happens in life.

In politics and in society today, we need more of this type of accountability. We need leaders to stand up and admit mistakes, to say they messed up, and then to tell us how they can do better. We need leaders to be transparent and open about what is going on and the decisions they made so that we can see where accountability lies.

Maintaining the balance in the paradox of accountability and delegation in any organization and family is a difficult path. The dynamics of the flow of both principles has to be a two-way street, where accountability and delegation flow down and up. It isn't enough in an organization to delegate downward and then have accountability move from top to bottom. Leaders must also allow room for accountability and delegation to flow upward. If someone in an organization needs help, they need to be given space to ask their leader for it.

Presidents and CEOs should implement ways to

provide avenues of accountability both from their offices and into their offices. They should hold people who work for them accountable as they delegate decision making, but they should also allow folks to hold the leader and others accountable for mismanagement.

Many CEOs and presidents tend to retain the real power in their Oval Office or C-suite, merely delegating responsibility outward. They take the credit for good things, and they blame others for the mistakes, while never giving authority away. If we are going to have a new way, this must change. People who work for you must be given enough runway to be creative and to make mistakes. When you do that, you have to accept that mistakes will be made. You can't manage people in a way that makes people afraid of taking risks and potentially screwing up.

Maybe you don't need a family trial to discover mistakes, delegate roles, or figure out accountability, but we each have to figure out the best avenue as leaders to practice both delegation and accountability simultaneously. One thing to remember, though: just don't light a stick standing over an open gas tank of a lawn mower. You will be held accountable, and you might not like the process it takes to get there.

CONCLUSION

Finding a new way for ourselves as leaders and as a country will not be easy or without challenge. It will require diligence, discipline, and determination to maintain the balance of all the required paradoxes. But doing so will enable us to thrive, live with purpose, and have a country and an economy that serves us all. We must be able to move into the future confidently while holding onto the values of old and the moments that shaped us into who we are today. I recall one of those moments for me from more than four decades ago.

Our family—I think there were nine of us children at the time—had just moved from Southfield, Michigan (a pretty standard, working-middle-class community just across the Detroit city line), to a much more affluent area called Bloomfield Hills. We had originally moved to

Southfield right before the riots in 1967, because my mom and pop wanted to make sure their kids weren't in danger. Then, right after we moved there, my pop would drive us down to Detroit as the riots unfolded. I clearly remember a tank parked in the middle of Woodward Avenue, which I thought was cool at the time. Now it seems tragic.

Our move to Bloomfield Hills, which, by most accounts, is one of the wealthiest areas in Michigan, felt a little like *The Beverly Hillbillies* show. We didn't have a truck like Jed and Granny Clampett loaded from top to bottom with all our possessions, but it was close. We certainly weren't aware of the expectations in a wealthy community like that. My parents didn't have a lot of money. They lived paycheck to paycheck and were raising a huge brood of children. They had been able to get a great deal on a piece of property, and they built a house that could keep us all comfortable under one roof.

We didn't have the clothes and haircuts and toys like everyone else had in this wealthy area, so we were picked on by many of the neighbors. My pop used to give each of us boys crew cuts next to the washing machine with an old bed sheet wrapped around us. Stylists weren't an option, as they were for everyone else in town. Many of the folks in Bloomfield Hills considered us low-class, unruly, and out of control, and they felt that we shouldn't be in their village. In fact, one neighbor built a six-foot-high fence within weeks of our moving in. There weren't any "Welcome to the neighborhood!" signs put up or any cakes brought over.

We lived near the railroad track. To this day, I still love the sound of railroads. Railroads to me have an incredible sense of wonder about them. It's as if they can take you anywhere, away from the sadness and troubles you feel. Or to some exciting far-off places of great wonder.

My siblings and I would play on the tracks and watch the trains go by. Sometimes we would even hop on as the trains moved slowly, ride them for a bit, pretending we were going to some exotic land, and jump off after less than a mile. We would find interesting items that flew off the trains, such as big packing bags that we would play on for hours. We would put coins on the track, watch them get smashed on the rails, and then save the flattened results as though we had just created some new currency.

Each morning I would walk the mile or so along the track to the junior high I attended. The best part of my day was the walk to school and home from school along those railroad tracks. I would get lost in the rhythm of jumping from railroad tie to railroad tie, or I would maintain my balance as I walked along the rail.

We had moved right before my seventh-grade year, a tough time to transition into a new community, moving from elementary school to the teen years. Being from a large family without a lot of money, we automatically got put into an "outsider" category. Kids aren't always the nicest or very accepting of outsiders or folks who don't fit in—especially if those folks have homemade haircuts. Teens can be abusive: name-calling, pushing, bullying, and all the other mean stuff that goes on. Back then there wasn't a lot of talk about bullying as there is today. It was just called "teasing" or "overly assertive behavior." I decided that I may not look the coolest, have the latest jeans or running shoes, or have a handsome haircut, but I was going to be one of the smartest kids in the school. Go ahead and judge me about everything else, but I will beat you at academics.

I made As in nearly every one of my classes throughout junior high and high school. I did the same in college. I learned very well the game of what teachers expected, and I played it back to them just the way they wanted. I never felt much pressure about school, because I realized how much of a competitive game it was. I read all the time, figured out the objectives of the teachers, and did what I needed to get by.

I soaked up books and knowledge as much as I possibly could. I got to be very good friends with the nerds in school. I guess I was one of them. I still had fun and got into some trouble, but the nerds felt more like me. They were (or should I say, "we were?") smart—but outcasts.

This all leads me to something that happened in seventh-grade social studies class.

We were studying the states and their capitals. There was a big test on this section. We had to write down all fifty states in order from memory, their capitals, and one fact about each state. That fact could be something like a state tree or rock or sporting team. I had studied, and I was ready. I knew it was just a memorization game, but it fascinated me, and to this day, I still try to remember every capital city. Even when I visit a state for the first time, I always try to go to the state capital. I guess old ways are hard to let go.

I received a blank piece of paper from the teacher, proceeded to write down all the states in alphabetical order, and then filled in each state with capitals and facts. The problem was for some unknown reason I couldn't remember the capital of New Jersey. It was a block in my mind. Kind of like the traffic jam that got Governor Chris Christie of New Jersey into so much hot water and doomed his career. I had every other piece of information down. I was missing only one piece of data.

So instead of just turning the paper in with 149 out of 150 pieces of info (which would have still been an incredibly high A), I turned around and asked a kid behind me what was the capital of New Jersey. He was going to make a C on his work, which was his normal grade, but he knew it was Trenton. He whispered it to me, I wrote it in, and I handed the paper to Mr. Johnson, our social studies teacher. The ironic thing is that the kid who gave me the answer smiled about it for weeks, since he'd given the "smart" kid an answer.

The next day Mr. Johnson handed back the graded tests

and announced to the class I had made the only perfect score. In fact, he said that no one else had gotten above 145 points. He was proud of me. He had me stand up in the front of the class, so I could be applauded and celebrated. (Again, all part of the game of school, which sometimes breeds unhealthy competition.) But I felt horrible, like absolute dog crap. I had gotten a perfect score, and it wasn't worth it. I wished I had gotten the 149 and had not cheated. It felt like I had failed that test.

Did I do the really honorable thing and go up to Mr. Johnson and admit that I had cheated? No. I was too scared, I guess. I wish I had. I did resolve that day to never cheat in school again, no matter what was at stake. I would take whatever score I was supposed to get and be satisfied with that.

It gives me some insight into how athletes such as Lance Armstrong or even politicians can get so caught up in the game. They want to be the best, and then they watch as their deep values slip away bit by bit. We are afraid of the consequences, so we keep protecting what we did.

Yes, I wanted to be one of the smartest kids in school. And yes, I had a chip on my shoulder because of all the other stuff about not fitting in or not having what everyone else at school had. One of the greatest things I ever learned was not that Trenton is the capital of New Jersey, but that getting a perfect score the wrong way sticks with you the rest of your life.

The process of finding a new way in life is a realization

that the values you have are so connected to your heart and soul that, if you lose them, then whatever you have on the surface—your job, hobbies, credentials, schooling, possessions—never suffices.

I haven't been perfect all of my life by any stretch of the imagination. I have made a number of mistakes. I have not always been honorable in my actions and interactions. But a test in seventh-grade social studies gave me an early lesson into how deeply we are affected when we lose our way. When we buy too much into the game we are playing and forget what really matters.

Throughout this book, I have tried to focus on what really matters. I want to share that embracing the paradox of competing values will help us chart a new way. I want us to move into the future without losing our compass, chartered by our hearts and souls. The paradoxes of Love, Truth, Surrender, Heart, Vision, Idealism, Openness, and Accountability become increasingly important to navigate if we want to be leaders who thrive.

I would now like to end with five practical applications or suggestions on how we might apply these lessons.

1. COUNTRY OVER PARTY

Starting with our political leaders in Washington, DC, but moving outward across America, it is key that we put the interests of our country over partisan concerns. It should not matter which jersey we each wear; we must put aside our party labels and make decisions that put our nation ahead of political gain. During President Obama's administration, we watched most Democrats line up for and most Republicans line up against in a reflexive knee-jerk fashion regardless of what principle was at stake. We are now seeing the same thing unfold in the Trump administration in the converse way: Republicans support him automatically, and Democrats oppose him no matter what.

Our founders warned against this numerous times. They wrote and spoke about the dangers of organizing in a partisan way or embracing tribal attitudes. This is what dooms democracies. We are in dire need of independent, commonsense thinking that enables us to come together for the common good regardless of political party.

It is not just incumbent on our leaders to practice this, but voters must begin to communicate and cast ballots that are not determined by party allegiance. Voters must show our leaders that they are tired of Republicans and Democrats putting their party over country. People who want Washington and state capitals to do something to help their industry should also weigh in not just on their particular concern but in a holistic way on what is best for the United States as a whole.

However, putting country over party is not just a practice for politics; it is a way of prioritizing what matters in America. We must demand that leaders of every organization put this brand into action. Business leaders should take the brand of country over party and apply it to their decisions. Maintaining a financially viable business is important, but businesses must have a brand that puts community over profit. This may mean taking an economic hit in the short run in order to make the best decision on behalf of employees and the community they live and work in. It is not enough anymore to follow the stock market as the only indicator of success. If our country is going to be prosperous in the decades ahead, it is crucial that our economic decision-making model allows room for businesses to put the interest of community above profit.

Further, both businesses and philanthropic endeavors should reflect on their highest missions. They must practice country over party when they deal with customers and clients. Service to customers and clients, as opposed to position, prominence, or profit, should be the North Star that guides us.

Leaders of these organizations must begin to practice what they preach through their mission. In their own lives and in their relationships with customers and coworkers, they need to live the values that they advocate. We are not a success if our customers and coworkers believe their interests are secondary to the whims of executives.

"Country over Party," "Community over Profit," and "Customer and Coworker over Personal Gain" are not just empty slogans. They need to be living, breathing methods we each practice every day.

2. A CODE

In his exceptional book, *Cowboy Ethics*, James Owen explains that cowboy ethics are a great barometer for how we might line up our lives today. In examining the Code of the West, Owen discusses such principles as taking pride in our work, being tough but fair, riding for the brand, talking less but saying more, etc. All these rules are applicable to yesterday, today, and tomorrow, whether we are wearing cowboy boots or Converse All Stars.

I would like to broaden this discussion to a degree and suggest, as leaders, it is imperative that we come up with our own "Code" of living. As we wade through all the paradoxes mentioned earlier, we each must figure out what are the principles of the Code that we want to live by. You are more than welcome to adopt the Code of the West that Mr. Owen lays out in his book or, as you read and talk to others, to adopt their Code to make your own. But I would counsel you to make sure the Code fits you in particular.

Another Code I discovered on the web for communicating was the acronym T.H.I.N.K. The acronym stands for the idea that before you say something or write something in communication with others, you should ask yourself if it is True, Helpful, Inspiring, Necessary, and Kind. I haven't consistently been successful at hitting on all five of those cylinders, but at least I try to hit on three of the five regularly.

What are the values you hold most dear? What are those

principles that you seem to always want others to adhere to? Oftentimes the things we criticize others about most frequently are signals of what our own Code of living and leadership needs to be. What upsets us in others is usually a sign of what we lack in ourselves; it tells us how we need to adhere to a Code.

Write some words down that matter to you—your qualities and values. Delve into what behavior touches you most pointedly. As you look at our president, leaders in Congress, CEOs, and folks running local organizations, what are the behaviors you applaud? Which ones do you think they could be better at? This will give you an indication of your Code. Then you can move that Code outside of yourself as you ask others to hold you accountable before you hold others accountable for their Codes.

Start with four or five principles of your Code. Expand it or subtract from it as you learn more about yourself and how you want to interact with the world. This Code can adjust as you go through life. You may not have the exact words today, but at least give it a start and see what you end up with. Then share it with others whom you trust and get their feedback. Ask them to help you stay in alignment.

One part of my own Code is to try to love unconditionally. It is tough, but it is the way our Almighty loves us. One day a while back, I came up with a revelation: God doesn't care if I love Him, He only cares that I know He loves me. He is God, by the way, so why would He need me to love

Him? He has all He needs. He is all He is. His promise to us is that He loves us. That is what we need to know.

I decided that this concept of universal love was something I should apply in my own circles. We must attempt to love unconditionally, not seeking love from another but making sure they know we love them. That type of love is transformative. This was the revelation that came out of my Code, a call to love grounded in my personal faith.

Besides loving unconditionally, my Code in part is to be a humble servant leader, to live a life of integrity, to know that good conquers evil, to treat others the way I want to be treated, to prefer being kind to being right, to leave my community better than when I came into it, to live simply to simply live, to be strong and gentle, and to trust others until they give you a reason not to. The Code will change. I will edit it as I go through the days and years ahead.

Without a Code, we all will get lost in the forest of this world. And leadership is supposed to help find the way.

3. GET OUT OF THE BUBBLE

Presidents, CEOs, and leaders of large organizations have a very difficult time getting outside of a small and insular group of people. They get cocooned in a comfortable environment, where everyone tells them how great they are. They begin making decisions without considering who will be widely impacted by those decisions. They have a false sense of reality.

Presidents and CEOs should regularly get out in the "field," out of the corner office or the Oval Office, and spend quality time with their consumers and employees. Not in a photo-op kind of way but in a substantive, real manner. A regular part of their week should be spent out in the real world, not in giving speeches or attending seminars or rallies.

As leaders, we should be engaging with those we typically view as our competitors or opponents. It would benefit the company or the country immensely if the leaders spent serious quality time with those they view as competitors. CEOs should begin to understand their company's overall mission more deeply so they can regard marketplace competitors as possible allies in accomplishing it.

These leaders could begin to build relationships that might alter the cutthroat tactics often employed. They may simultaneously learn from their competitors to improve at their own jobs. The president should do the same with leaders in the opposite party. He or she might set up an office in the US Capitol and spend regular time there building relationships. The most underused power of the White House in the past twenty years is the social presidency. Leaders must build relationships for relationship's sake and not merely for temporary transactional purposes.

As part of moving out of insular circles, figuring out ways to move decision-making structures more locally is key for CEOs and presidents. There is no reason that federal or state government structures and programs have to be so Washington- or state-capital-centric. Many of the programs could be better implemented as community-based programs. Why can't we organize some federal and state programs in local schools, which today are an underutilized asset (these incredible spaces sit empty on weekends and after school)? Federal or state employees could interact with citizens in a more neighborly fashion.

CEOs must realize that innovation and employee morale are best enhanced with operations that are more decentralized. Consumers will see the benefit of the business more clearly. With technology, the ease of travel and communication mean that executives no longer need to be side by side in an office building. Broaden the definition of headquarters.

4. NATIONAL SERVICE

Business, political, and philanthropic leaders need to find ways to enhance a sense of community among their employees, consumers, and citizens. There is a series of great challenges facing our country and this world. Implementing some level of national service expectation will feed the hunger for connection and meaning. There are many highly successful organizations, such as City Year (which my youngest son, Jacob, and my niece and goddaughter were involved with in Miami and San Jose), where needs are met with government, schools, and businesses cooperating.

One of the major missed opportunities of President Obama was that in his historical 2008 presidential campaign, he motivated millions of young people to vote and get involved enthusiastically. But, after getting elected, he never gave them an outlet of service to engage in and to channel that energy in a way that wasn't just political but that made our communities and our country a better place. This youth energy quickly dissipated without that White House call to action. This generation wasn't interested in a specific policy, but in change. When they didn't see Washington changing, they were left disappointed, dissatisfied, and disengaged, as was reflected in low turnouts among young people in the 2016 election.

Leaders throughout the United States, including our new president, should call for a mission of national service for all Americans, young or old; all of us should be given the opportunity to serve for at least a year in some public service capacity. CEOs of companies and philanthropies could be directly involved in making this happen, freeing up their employees to take time away from their jobs to engage in this mission.

We should fully fund such service opportunities through allocating tax dollars, soliciting business contributions, or channeling charitable dollars. There are too many people today who want an opportunity to help, but there are too few spots available for this kind of service. It could be in the military or in domestic or international service projects. Everyone should be expected to be a part of this initiative in some way. Employers and governments at all levels should support this fully.

It is these national service opportunities that will significantly help us get out of the self-centeredness many of us too often default into. We can begin to bridge the divides so we can all come together as one team. This program could give us a purpose and meaning in our lives that will only make the country and the world a better place.

5. FUN

While we are balancing the key paradoxes, putting together a daily practice to stay disciplined in our leadership and life direction, establishing a Code, and being of service, we must not forget that our short and precious time on this planet is meant to be fun. Enjoyment and laughter and fun are essential elements of success—especially in this serious world, which seems to bear down on us and our organizations on an hourly basis. Those leaders and organizations that enjoy what they are doing, have fun in their work, and wake up every day welcoming a challenge with a smile will be the ones you can bet will triumph.

In 2004, some media folks came by the Bush presidential reelection campaign headquarters in Virginia and wanted an update on what was going on. We went through polls and analyses of all the tactics and messaging of the campaign. At the end of the presentation, I suggested the best indicator of who was going to win: walk through both of the campaign headquarters and see who is having the most fun. See where the most laughter is, and that candidate will likely be your winner. A couple of weeks later, two of the media folks came back and said, "We walked through both Kerry's campaign and yours, and you all are by far having the most fun." For many voters in 2016, they saw Donald Trump and his campaign having more fun than Hillary Clinton's effort, and they responded to this emotion. I call this the Southwest Airlines theory of success.

Southwest Airlines, based in Dallas, Texas, and one of the most successful companies, has fun, and you can feel their enjoyment. Listen to their pilots, flight attendants, and gate attendants. They are all enjoying their day, their interactions with customers, and one another. And we can feel it. It might not be the "first class" travel that some people want, but it is an experience you will enjoy. It is a big reason why they are profitable. Southwest cares about their employees and customers. They are having fun.

The best leaders have a sense of humor, not through jokes, sarcasm, or bitter wit but by conveying the sense that they are doing serious stuff without taking themselves too seriously. We each need to find where the fun is, as a child might do, and there we will find success.

One more final personal story that touches on fun and the joys of the journey ahead.

When you grow up with six brothers and four sisters in Detroit as part of a crazy Irish Catholic family, there are a variety of avenues of fun and distraction. Especially without social networking, video games, online chats, or 786 cable channels.

I remember so well the day we finally got our first color television set (this was in the late 1970s). My father was so worried we kids would damage it that he put it up near the ceiling corner of the family room by the fireplace. Like you would see in a doctor's or dentist's office.

And since there was no remote control around, we kids had to stand on the hearth of the fireplace to try to change the channels. We would switch between the four or five channels we could get, which included a Canadian channel from Windsor. Usually one of the siblings was designated as the channel changer so the rest of us could relax. As you might guess, we didn't spend a lot of time in front of the tube. So, in those days, we went looking for creative ways to horse around and engage our brothers and sisters in some "harmless" fun.

Hence, the creation of a game one of us dubbed "Bumbly Bee." Every game invented needs a unique name. The name brands the game. It makes it easier to suggest when you want to play it again or tell the story of the last time you played. Besides, it seems to be in the human condition to name things. Businesses, nicknames, or dreams. This particular game name of Bumbly Bee will become clearer as I go on.

And so, after having exhausted all the other ball games, swing sets, and dirt bomb fights (this is a game where you pick sides and throw clods of dirt at one another), we turned to different pursuits.

The game of Bumbly Bee starts with taking old dishrags from under the kitchen sink and then tying them together as tightly as possible in the form of a ball the size of a softball. You would tie these old rags into a series of knots that would make one larger knot. This is best done at night (preferably a Friday or Saturday night) because of the next dangerous and troubling step involved (and because it is easier to sneak the rags from your mom at the end of a long day).

This ball of rags is then soaked overnight in a coffee can filled with gasoline. Gasoline became a go-to valuable item in those days. We tried charcoal fluid, but it just didn't have the same impact in the game the next morning. With the rags soaking, we could go to sleep and dream of playing the game in the morning.

After it had a good overnight soaking, we would empty the gasoline-soaked rag ball out onto an open lawn area, not in the line of sight of the windows of the house or of any neighbors who might be watching. Now the game was about to begin. We would need at least four or five people to gather around the ball at this point. It was time to play Bumbly Bee. We lit the gasoline ball, and everyone made a mad scramble to kick the flaming orb.

The mission of the game was to kick the flaming ball at one another so that it hit someone. If you got hit and it left a flame spot on your clothes, you were out for that round. If it missed you or if your contact with the ball didn't leave a flame mark on you, then you got to stay in the game. The game continued until only one person was left, and that person was the winner of that particular round. This went on for a few rounds until the gasoline burned out and all you had left were burnt rags. There was no ultimate winner, because different people took different rounds, so the point of the game was to laugh and survive as long as you could.

I know many of you are thinking, "These folks were totally messed up and out of control" or "Where were their parents?" Both of these are valid points. There are probably other judgments to be made, as well as a very key question about the parents. But heck, with eleven kids running around, stuff was going to happen out of eyesight of the wardens.

First, when you are part of a large family without nannies or housekeepers, then it is a bit of a *Lord of the Flies* upbringing. You learn self-reliance, creativity, spontaneity, and survival techniques. Sure, there are a few trips to the emergency room and, later, chats with psychologists, therapy sessions, and self-help groups.

Second, even in this craziness, we did have structure and rules. It was kind of funny in this bizarre game that there was still a form to the play and there were certain rules that needed to be abided by. It wasn't like the unstructured and without-rhyme-or-reason fun of throwing rocks at windows or pushing trash cans down hills (all of which we also did, but it didn't seem as much fun). It was the structure that gave the game meaning and true competitive joy.

Even in our unfettered fun, we as human beings are best equipped to play in games with set rules and a real structure. You know when those rules are violated. Even in this lunatic game, structure gave the time a feeling of integrity and meaning. And it is that integrity and meaning that enables one to live life fully, I believe. As human beings we love freedom, but we also crave structure.

At times, just crazy unstructured fun is important and freeing. Without constraint or rules, you can feel free and exuberant and open. But the terms of play and the rules involved in games give a little more meaning to your life. I think this is especially true when you can create the rules on your own and implement them in the moment. Rules imposed by others can be good and a guidepost at times, but sometimes those rules need to be broken in order for you to grow.

We desire freedom, but we also need the security of some structure and rules under which we operate. We need some common basis of values that we retain within our own lives and then share with others in the community. In that common bond, we have respect for others and hold one another accountable. The values of the thousands of years of civilization are still integral for humanity, but we need to set up some new rules upon which we relate to one another.

This book is my attempt in fleshing out a new way forward for leaders at all levels. Each of us needs to figure out what gives us meaning in our own lives, where our hearts demand that we go, and how we best serve a broader goal. We come from diverse family backgrounds, we have unique talents and strengths, we carry with us our own responsibilities and commitments, but we are all trying to find our way home. We are all looking for a new way in an evolving world.

The path ahead doesn't have to involve running for office, but it does require us not running from ourselves. It doesn't necessarily mean being a high-level manager, but it does mean each of us managing to get to a higher place. The ebb and flow of our own stories, where we come from, the messages that come from our own hearts and souls, will help give us direction to be the leaders in our own lives.

We will each have to figure out the balance of the many paradoxes of life and leading. It is in that tension we can discover a new way. In finding a new way for each of our own worlds, we can find the way for the whole wide world. As my daughter said to me when she was very young, "I love you, Daddy, whole wide world." My hope is we each can embrace the power and love that is so abundant in us and around us. As individuals and as a world, we can find our way to a new American home.

Oh—why was it called Bumbly Bee? That is the fascinating part. When the flaming ball of rags is kicked at you, misses your actual body parts, and glides very close to your ear, it gives off the sound of a bumble bee flying. I don't recommend trying to prove that on your own; just trust me on that one.

Because, after all, life is about not only the momentous things—forty-day pilgrimages and moments of change for our nation and births and deaths and love—but also the small things—playing strange games with your large family or receiving love notes from your tiny daughter. Life is made both in the big moments and in the small moments in between. Life itself is a paradox. Onward.

There you have it.

MATTHEW DOWD is the *New York Times* best-selling coauthor of *Applebee's America* and chief analyst for ABC News. He is the founder of four companies and ListenTo. Us, a community of independent-minded folks interested in commonsense leadership. He has been a strategist for CEOs and politicians on both sides of the aisle, but today is a die-hard independent. He was born in Detroit and now lives in central Texas.

CPSIA information can be obtained
at www.ICGtesting.com
Printed in the USA
FSOW03n2115260417
33608FS